Teach Smart

11 Learner-Centered Strategies That Ensure Student Success

PJ Caposey and Todd Whitaker

Routledge
Taylor & Francis Group

NEW YORK AND LONDON

First published 2014
by Routledge
711 Third Avenue, New York, NY 10017

Simultaneously published in the UK
by Routledge
2 Park Square, Milton Park, Abingdon, Oxon OX14 4RN

Routledge is an imprint of the Taylor & Francis Group, an informa business

Library of Congress Cataloging-in-Publication Data

Caposey, P. J.
Teach smart : 11 learner-centered strategies that ensure student success/
PJ Caposey and Todd Whitaker.
    pages   cm
1. Student-centered learning.
I. Whitaker, Todd. II. Title.
LB1027.23.C18 2013
371.39'4—dc23   2013008656

ISBN: 978-1-59667-249-9 (pbk)

Typeset in Palatino and Formata
by click! Publishing Services
Cover Designer: Dave Strauss/3FoldDesign

SUSTAINABLE
FORESTRY
INITIATIVE

Certified Sourcing
www.sfiprogram.org
SFI-00555
The SFI label applies to the text stock.

Printed and bound in the United States of America by
Walsworth Publishing Company, Marceline, MO.

This book was written in honor of the educators who have had a tremendous impact on our lives—both as our teachers and colleagues—in hopes that we may have an impact on them and all educators to better support the growth of children.

Meet the Authors

 **PJ Caposey** has had a wide range of educational experiences throughout his career. His educational career began when he received the Golden Apple Scholarship in high school, which supports students as they pursue their dream to teach by providing scholarship money and training in return for a commitment to teach in a need-based area. PJ did just that after completing his studies at Eastern Illinois University by teaching at Percy Lavon Julian High School in the inner city of Chicago.

After completing his administrative certification at National Louis University, PJ served as an assistant principal in the Rockford Public Schools before becoming the principal of Oregon High School at the age of 28. Since he arrived at Oregon High School, PJ and the school have received many honors, including winning the Illinois Principals Association/Horace Mann Partners in Education Award, and being named one of the nation's top high schools by *US News and World Report*. PJ personally has been selected as an Award of Merit winner by the Those Who Excel program sponsored by the Illinois State Board of Education, and he was recently honored as one of the nation's top young educators when named an Honoree for the ASCD Outstanding Young Educator Award.

Currently, PJ is pursuing his doctoral degree through Western Illinois University. He continues to write and guest blog for many websites, including Eye On Education, ASCD, Edutopia, My Town Tutors, and Test Soup. PJ has also become a sought after presenter, consultant, and professional development provider and has spoken at many local, state, and national conferences. He has served in different consultative capacities for schools and other organizations. In addition, PJ serves as an adjunct professor for Aurora University within their educational leadership department. PJ also is committed to staying connected as an educator; he can be followed on twitter @principalpc and many of his personal writings and communications are shared through his personal website at www.pjcaposey.com

PJ is married to a teacher who works with gifted students. They live with their two sons, Jameson and Jackson, in the Northwestern part of Illinois.

Dr. Todd Whitaker has been fortunate to be able to blend his passion with his career. Recognized as a leading presenter in the field of education, his message about the importance of teaching has resonated with hundreds of thousands of educators around the world. Todd is a professor of educational leadership at Indiana State University in Terre Haute, Indiana, and he has spent his life pursuing his love of education by researching and studying effective teachers and principals.

Prior to moving into higher education, he was a math teacher and basketball coach in Missouri. Todd then served as a principal at the middle school, junior high, and high school levels. He was also a middle school coordinator in charge of staffing, curriculum, and technology for the opening of new middle schools.

One of the nation's leading authorities on staff motivation, teacher leadership, and principal effectiveness, Todd has written more than 30 books, including the national best seller, *What Great Teachers Do Differently*. Other titles include: *Shifting the Monkey, Dealing With Difficult Teachers, 10 Minute Inservice, The Ball, What Great Principals Do Differently, Motivating & Inspiring Teachers, and Dealing With Difficult Parents.*

Todd is married to Beth, also a former teacher and principal, who is a professor of elementary education at Indiana State University. They are the parents of three children; Katherine, Madeline, and Harrison.

Acknowledgments

One thing that binds humans together is that we are all learners—
throughout our entire lives. I think the best way that I can say thank you
to people is to simply acknowledge that I am who I am as a result of the
wonderful teachers I have had throughout my life. Some of those teachers
stood at the front of the classroom each day, some were coaches, some were
family members, and others were just acquaintances. In addition, some of
the most important lessons I have learned came from my students, from
my children, and from observing the innocence of the young. Teachers are
all around us, and we are all similar in the fact that our lives have been
made better as a result of our teachers, mentors, coaches, students, parents,
or children. For everyone who sets forth each day to make a contribution
to the learning of a child—thank you.

As for my personal teachers in my profession and in my life: Thank you
to my wife, Jacquie; my sons, Jameson and Jackson; my family—Dad, Ma,
Nina, Nanny, Grandpa, the two Kevins, and Jolene; my friend and mentor
Tom Mahoney; and my co-author Todd Whitaker. I am who I am because
of you—this book exists more because of you than it does because of me.
Many thanks . . .

Table of Contents

Introduction

Imagine you are playing a carnival game in which you must throw a softball and attempt to knock over some glass jars. In order to win a prize, you must knock over 15 of the 30 jars from 10 feet away. Some jars are wobbly and easy to knock over, and others are glued to the table and have to be struck just perfectly. You are not told which ones are stuck to the table and which ones are easy to knock down. Now, imagine that after you throw the first set of balls, you are asked to repeat the process. This, time, however, you have to stand another five feet back, and you must knock down 17 of the 30 jars. Once you are done, you have to try again from the same distance, but you must use a pellet gun and knock over 20 jars. Later, you are given the same task, but you are timed. This continues again and again, with new additions or modifications each time. By the tenth time, you have a strong pellet gun with a scope, but you are 20 feet away, the majority of the jars are glued to the table, and you must knock over all 30 jars to win a prize. This game no longer sounds fun, does it? But this is the game teachers have been asked to play over the past two decades.

For teachers, the bar continues to be raised as the country's demographics keep changing, the quantification of success keeps changing, and the tools with which to accomplish the goals keep changing, too. Although individual teachers and schools may have little control over the rules of the game in terms of the overall educational landscape, they do have a great deal of control over how they approach the contest. In the above scenario, it would be easy for the contestants to become focused on a variety of things. They could become consumed with the mechanics of how they throw the ball, how well they implement the tools they are given, or how difficult or unfair the task is, since the jars are glued to the table. The ones who will be the most successful are the ones consumed with one thought—getting the jars to fall.

The same holds true for teachers. As teachers, it may seem impossible to keep up with the legislative and philosophical changes that have been dominating the educational landscape over the past two decades. From the passing of No Child Left Behind, to the Common Core State Standards, to evaluation system overhauls, to the influx of technology leading to one-to-one initiatives and the prominent use of social media in the classroom, it *seems* as though the job of teachers is much different than it has ever been before.

This book is to serve as a reminder that the job of teachers, while immensely difficult, has not changed. In its simplest form, the job of teachers is to help learners learn. The measure of success may constantly change, the tools with which kids are educated may constantly change, and the process may get more challenging each year, but as educators, we have to stay focused on our primary purpose: helping kids achieve academic growth.

Why We Wrote This Book

The impetus for writing this book was a conversation we enjoyed with colleagues. As a group of administrators and former administrators, we were discussing our successes and failures in helping teachers move forward and grow professionally. As the conversation progressed, the question around the table became this: Was there a common denominator among those teachers in our buildings who were experiencing success compared to those who were struggling to progress?

The conversation was fruitful and in the end our answer was yes—and it was quite simple. The teachers whose classrooms, lessons, and planning focused on the *kids* above all else were greatly successful. The teachers whose actions were dominated by rules, policies, content, and other adult-centered paradigms were experiencing a lack of professional growth and struggling to move students forward.

As a collective group, we began seeking out the best literature to help us support our staff members who needed to become learner-centered. The literature we found was lacking, and it was particularly lacking in concrete ways in which a teacher could transform daily actions from a traditional, teacher-centered paradigm to a progressive, learner-centered model. With the lack of literature available, it became clear that we needed to write a guidebook outlining a variety of helpful learner-centered strategies.

Who Should Read This Book

Our primary intent in writing this book was to provide teachers seeking to improve their professional practice with concrete examples of how to transform common, everyday practice into meaningful, learner-centered best practices. Our belief is that reading the book in its entirety will help teachers not only transform their practices, but also align their actions and behaviors to the core purpose of why they are educators—to support the growth and learning of children. The organization of the book will, however, also allow teachers to pick up the book, consult a particular chapter, and transform a singular component of their professional practice.

This book can also serve multiple purposes for school leaders. First and foremost, many administrators still have personal doubts when it comes to serving as their school's instructional leader. This book not only provides background on effective learner-centered strategies but also explains why these strategies work. As is evident throughout the book, learner-centered behaviors are also best-practice methodologies. Learning about them will thus deepen the breadth of an administrator's knowledge. In addition, this book will serve as a guide to administrators working on professional growth plans with their teachers. This book can also be used in book studies to help shift a school's culture from rule-centered or adult-centered to truly learner-centered.

We believe that the most successful schools in the nation, whether they are 90/90/90 schools or are recognized by *U.S. News and World Report*, are learner-centered in their approach to the educational process. Teaching smart—putting students at the center of your instruction—will help them achieve greater academic and personal growth. Enjoy the journey!

STRATEGY

Begin on Day One

If you are from the "Don't let them see you smile until November" crowd, this chapter will challenge your thinking. The first days of school mark an exciting and exhausting time that is essential for setting the tone within the classroom. Before we get into this chapter's strategy, I would like each teacher reading this book to imagine that it is the first faculty meeting of the year and a new principal was hired over the summer. (Some of you should not be smiling as big as you are.) Ask yourselves the question, "What could he or she do to really win me over—to convince me that he or she is truly concerned with my success above all else?" That question is important, because if teachers leave the first meeting of the year with the belief that their administration truly values their success, the school is destined for a great year. The classroom is no different—if kids truly believe that their teacher is committed to their success, they will have a great year. And just as a new principal has only one chance to set a positive tone at the opening faculty meeting, you the teacher have only one chance to set the tone for your students during the first week of school. In both situations, it is important to get it right!

The Common Reality

Teachers have a lot of "stuff" to do during the first week of school. On top of the "stuff," the days are usually shortened to some extent, and the purpose of the week (or what it should be) gets lost. Following is a list of things that we have found—through observation and professional dialogue—to be the focus of the average Day One or Week One of the school year:

- ◆ Create seating chart.
- ◆ Go over expectations and consequences.
- ◆ Hand out all necessary paperwork (syllabus, etc.) and discuss.
- ◆ Give paperwork to kids to take home for a parent signature.
- ◆ Hand out textbooks or other supplies.

Let's revisit the analogy to the first faculty meeting of the year. If the principal spends the meeting discussing the faculty handbook and how you may be written-up if you do not comply, does that create the feeling that he is vested in your personal growth and success as an educator? If your answer is no, then this type of practice should not be what takes place on the first days of school.

Example of Excellence

In education, it is vital to not become bogged down with negativity about professional practice. Our assumption and hope is that there are pockets of outstanding learner-centered practices taking place in every school building throughout the country. We think it is important that in each chapter, we refer to these examples of excellence to provide insight into the chapter's strategy and also to provide reassurance to all teachers reading that this really is possible. Yes, you can do it!

Mrs. Foster is a kindergarten teacher who has taught in the same building for more than 25 years. When people talk about her in the little town where she teaches, she is credited "for raising half of the town." On the first day of school, she pushes all of the desks to the side of the room and has the children sit in a circle on what will be the reading rug. She has the students introduce themselves, and she participates as well. After everybody has been introduced, Mrs. Foster asks a "closed" question such as, "What is your favorite color?" The students respond and are grouped accordingly. Once grouped, the students are asked an open-ended question such as, "What was the best thing you did over the summer?" While the kids work in their groups, Mrs. Foster moves about the classroom and discusses how group members should interact. Once the conversations die down, the students are given paper and other supplies to draw the activity.

They are asked to write their name on the top right-hand corner. Students are also told that if they want to write about the activity, they can do that on the back of the sheet. Once this activity is complete, students are asked if they can line up in alphabetical order. The students often struggle with this, but with some facilitating they can complete the activity. Mrs. Foster then articulates how to line up in a single file, and she proceeds to move the desks back and have students sit in alphabetical order. Next, she explains to the students how excited she is because as a result of their hard work and her support, at the end of the year each student will be able to "count to 50, read 40 different words, tie their shoes," etc. For the final task of the day, Mrs. Foster hands each student a pre-made folder with all necessary paperwork. She asks them to please take it home to their parents.

Let's dissect Mrs. Foster's activities and what makes them so effective.

- ◆ Students feel safe and are asked to share their likes and dislikes.
- ◆ Students are able to work in randomly assigned groups and potentially make new friends.
- ◆ The teacher is able to establish norms for the classroom without taking class time or making it the explicit point of the lesson.
- ◆ The teacher gets to learn about the students and what they did over the summer.
- ◆ The teacher is able to assess students' pre-existing levels during a "fun" assignment.
- ◆ Students "work" to create their own seating chart and implicitly learn how to line up appropriately.
- ◆ Students are informed of their academic expectations in a positive manner that links the teacher as a support to their future success.
- ◆ Paperwork activities were completed ahead of time, and students are simply asked to work as a delivery system for such materials; instructional time is not wasted

Why This Is a Learner-Centered Strategy

The focus of Mrs. Foster's lesson is entirely on the students. The intent of the lesson is clear: students communicate with each other in order to form a sense of community within the classroom. In simpler terms, the desired outcome is for students to feel safe in the classroom. While achieving that primary goal, the teacher is also able to establish norms in the classroom, create a seating chart, and collect data on students' present levels of ability. In other words, the goals of traditional models of teaching are still accomplished (seating, paperwork, norms), but learner-centered strategies allow for additional depth of learning, better teacher/student relationships, and an increased focus on our true purpose.

How You Can Transform Your Practice

Before you can change your practice, you must analyze and evaluate what you're currently doing in the classroom. You also need to consider what truly needs to be accomplished during the first days of school. As an example, let's revisit the most common practices on the first day of school. Figure 1.1 (below) lists these practices. Read them and use them as a model for self-analysis.

Figure 1.1 Common Practices for the First Day of School

Current practice	What is this current practice truly attempting to accomplish?	What learner-centered practice could accomplish the same goal?
Giving out a seating chart	1. Allows for ease in learning names, passing back homework, etc. 2. Creates a normal distribution of kids to avoid potential discipline issues caused by kids sitting near friends	1. Don't use a chart the first day; take a survey instead. 2. Survey asks students whom they work well with, if there is a particular part of the room in which they prefer to sit, etc. OR 3. Have students sit with a strategic grouping based on previously collected data.
Going over expectations and consequences	1. Establishes norms of behavior 2. Establishes "who is boss"	1. Come up with student-created norms for behavior (through a discussion or in writing). 2. Teach norms for behavior implicitly and through direct conversation when needed.
Distributing and discussing paperwork	1. Provides all relevant information to students as directed by administration and makes sure you are protected moving forward 2. Gives rationale for grade assignments	1. Set clear outcomes for students, allowing them to understand what it will take for them to have success in the classroom.

Elements of a Learner-Centered Day One Lesson

Let's break down the elements of an effective learner-centered lesson for the first week of school. Effective lessons during the first week of school should include these elements:

- ◆ Community building
- ◆ Student sharing
- ◆ Surveys
- ◆ Norms
- ◆ Dual-purpose products
- ◆ Purpose of class
- ◆ Dual ownership of success

The other "stuff" that commonly takes place on an opening day is not truly necessary and should not require academic time. Seating charts are unnecessary unless they benefit kids, and there is no way to know that on the first days of school. Similarly, reading every sentence of handouts that are to be sent home should be discontinued unless reading each sentence improves the experience, behavior, or performance of the learner.

Community Building

The classroom environment should be defined by respect and rapport. In this environment, kids are comfortable engaging in critical thought and discussing their opinions, and are comfortable with being wrong and occasionally failing upon first try. These things do not just occur. Kids from age five to eighteen do not naturally have the confidence and courage to engage in all of these best practice activities. What is important to remember is that while these things do not occur naturally, all kids have the capacity for this to occur in any number of diverse settings. Building a community within your classroom, however, is similar to building a team and takes intentional effort from the teacher. In the following section, we outline three activities to build community. Each has its own benefits and detriments depending on your teaching style and personal preference, but all serve to promote the same end.

Concept One: Create Classroom-Wide Goals
In the same manner in which good administrators involve teachers in the goal-development process, so too do good teachers involve students in creating learning goals. Involving students allows the teacher to unveil what is to be learned and how it is to be assessed, and it allows students to determine what success means in their classroom. The teacher can work with students to create a classroom-wide goal. For instance, a goal can be that 85 percent of kids in the classroom will demonstrate proficiency on all standards addressed, or

92% of kids will earn a B+ or higher, or any other collaboratively established goal. Once a goal is set, the teacher can remind students that committing to a goal means they must be willing to support their classmates' learning. This process unites the students toward a common end immediately and should be referred to whenever classroom norms need to be reinforced.

Concept Two: Build Community Through Grouping

Student groupings are established via information shared with the class. This can be as simple as asking students how they learn best: through hearing, seeing, moving, or doing. Once you have their answers, create diverse groupings and explain to students that each member of their group has unique strengths and that throughout the year/quarter/month, each member will need to depend on another group member's strength to achieve maximum success.

Concept Three: Share and Model

This concept revolves around sharing and modeling. Simply having students engage in an activity that requires each person to share, including the teacher, begins the gradual climb toward community. Teachers can participate at any point (beginning, middle, or end) of the activity, depending on personal preference. For the activity to have maximum impact, the teacher must answer the same questions students are asked to respond to and open themselves up to a place of vulnerability. This looks different in second grade than it does it ninth because of levels of appropriateness, but sharing, modeling, and making yourself vulnerable in the classroom is a powerful lesson for students to observe.

Student Sharing

In most schools, students are expected to talk on the first day of school, in every one of their classes. Common first day questions include these:

♦ What's your name?
♦ What's your favorite subject?
♦ What's something fun you did this summer?

While there is nothing wrong with those questions, they can be improved upon if you add depth and if your questions make students take a "safe-risk" by answering them. Questions that can be considered include these:

♦ What was your best experience in school?
♦ What was your worst experience in school?
♦ What was one thing a teacher did that helped you learn the most?
♦ What was the one thing you have learned that you are the most proud of?

- ◆ What is the biggest obstacle you have ever had to overcome in school?
- ◆ What is your biggest hope for this year?
- ◆ What is one thing you are scared about being a _____ grader?

You can also provide a list such as the one above and ask the class to pick two questions to answer. This provides an increasingly safe environment for everybody in the classroom. To make this activity even more meaningful, tell students that they can't answer by just repeating what the person before them said (e.g., "What Johnny said"). This activity also provides the teacher with additional data to help facilitate learning in the future. Imagine the power of saying to a student in mid-November, "Remember when you told me about Mr. Zielinski and when he helped you figure out how to do long division? I am going to work with you as long as it takes until you understand comma splices as well as you do long division."

Surveys

By asking students questions in a non-threatening manner, we can learn a great deal about them as people and as students. With that type of information, teachers can better tailor instruction, intervention, or enrichment to meet the needs of each student. Questions that can be asked in a first-day survey include these:

1. What did your favorite teacher do differently to make him/her your favorite?
2. What did your least favorite teacher do differently to make him/her your least favorite?
3. When a teacher teaches something and you learn it very quickly, what is he/she doing that is different than the rest of the time?
4. When a teacher teaches something and it is hard for you to learn, what is he/she doing that is different from the rest of the time?
5. What is the best part about working in groups? What are the qualities of other students that you work best with?
6. What is the worst part about working in groups? What are the qualities of other students that you do not work well with?
7. Do you learn well on a computer? Tell me about something you learned and why it was easier on the computer.
8. Describe what you think of school in one word.
9. What is one thing I really need to know about you to be the best teacher to you that I can be?
10. When you get frustrated with learning a new concept, how would you like the teacher to interact with you—leave you alone for a minute, talk to you in the hallway, work with you individually inside the class, let your parents know so they can help you, etc.?

Using this simple list of ten questions will allow for much greater insight than the traditional opening-day activities, and it will enable you to adapt traditional practice in order to better meet the needs of kids. Feel free to add your own questions, too.

Norms

At the beginning of the year, it is necessary to establish what is expected and appropriate within the classroom. Establishing expectations, when examined in a vacuum, does not present as very learner-centered. However, with a few purposeful adjustments to the norm, it certainly can be. For this to be effective, you have to trust two things: 1) students really want a comfortable and well-behaved learning environment, and 2) you as teachers have the skills to lead and shape discussion. Teachers should enter this dialogue with students with an end in mind, and that end should consist of as few rules/norms as possible. During the dialogue, every student's voice must be heard and every student's propositions should be considered. Having led this activity and watched it many times, I can say that it is almost always possible to come away with this all-encompassing norm: Respect × 4:

- ◆ Respect yourselves.
- ◆ Respect your classmates.
- ◆ Respect me.
- ◆ Respect the classroom environment.

I sincerely believe that anything more than that is overkill. Any behavior associated with positive classroom interactions can be chunked into one of those four categories. If this process or this respect list does not meet your style as an educator, I implore you to do one thing: please refrain from listing rules as "Do not" statements, such as "Do not talk when I am talking." Those kinds of statements are power-driven and run counter to a student-centered environment.

Dual-Purpose Products

A teacher's goal during the opening days of the school year should be to establish a learner-centered environment, to gain as much information about kids as possible, and to enter into the curriculum of the class at first opportunity. As we discussed earlier in the chapter, there are many administrative tasks that need to occur during the first few days of class that often become the focus for teachers, and valuable time with students is not maximized. By carefully constructing a dual-purpose product that relates to the curriculum and is personal for students, teachers can accomplish many things. First, they can assess students' prior knowledge of content through the prompt. Second, they can create time to tackle some administrative tasks while students are meaningfully engaged. Next, they can construct the prompt in a manner that allows them to gain a better understanding of their students' personal likes and dislikes. Lastly, by having students create a product, teachers can gain insight into each student's skills within a content area, independent of prior knowledge. Following are some examples of prompts. As always, this list is not meant to be all-inclusive but is intended to prompt learner-centered thinking and help you create your own meaningful prompts for your classes.

Prompts for kindergarten through third grade:
♦ Write about your favorite activity from the summer and why it was your favorite.
♦ Tell me about the person you look up to the most.
♦ Tell me about your favorite TV show and favorite character.
♦ What is your favorite thing to do outside and why?

Prompts for fourth through eighth grade:
♦ Tell me about a time when you explored or investigated something and what you found.
♦ If you could build anything, what would it be?
♦ What things happened throughout the world since we left for summer break?
♦ Tell me about your favorite book and favorite character.

Prompts for ninth through twelfth grade:
♦ If you could have a meal with any two historical figures, who would they be and why?
♦ What is the most important invention in the last 50 years and why?
♦ What character in a work of art have you found to be most like you?
♦ How do you think this class will help you with what you want to do in the future?

Purpose of Class

Using carrots and sticks as motivators is so last century. For 21st-century work, leaders must motivate through autonomy, mastery, and purpose (Pink, 2009). It is ineffective to tell students that a particular grade, class, or subject is important simply because you (or someone else) said so or because it is a graduation requirement or moving-up requirement. Highly-effective, learner-centered classrooms are characterized by high expectations by both the students and teacher. The only way this is possible is if the teacher, from day one, expresses the purpose and value of what students will be learning.

This message, or statement of purpose, must be sincere to be effective. Preparing to deliver your message—which can be used throughout the year—requires you to reflect on why your subject is necessary for students to learn. Most educators know that what they do is important, but actually working through the process of articulating *why* it is important can be invigorating and inspiring.

Dual Ownership of Success

I am entering my fourth year as principal at my current school, and I sincerely believe that if a teacher who is committed to improving his or her professional practice and who is open to critique receives a negative evaluation, then it is as much my responsibility as that teacher's. If somebody is willing to develop and my job is to lead the process, then failure to move forward is both of our responsibilities. The same is true within the classroom. Teachers are successful based on student learning and the teacher's ability to move students forward. This is the core of being a learner-centered teacher.

Communicating this to students unites a classroom in a common purpose. The classroom can no longer be perceived as students versus the material or students versus the teacher; it becomes students and the teacher versus the desired outcome. Once students know that they are not struggling through this process alone and that their teacher's actions (not just on the first days) support this sentiment, a learner-centered environment is established and massive amounts of learning can take place.

Communicate for Your Audience

It is hard to imagine a single profession in which communication is not an integral part of job success. Educators are no exception. The title of this chapter is important because everybody communicates *to* their audience, but very few people communicate *for* their audience. Simply changing one word transforms the entire premise of communication as one driven by the producer (speaker) to the consumer (listener). This is an important concept to consider before delving into the chapter. Before we can begin, we must answer the question, "Do I communicate for me or for my audience?"

The Common Reality

Teachers have a tremendous amount of material to teach. In fact, noted researcher Robert Marzano estimates that in order to teach everything described in content area standards, kids would have to be in primary and secondary schools for more than 20 years (Marzano & Kendall, 1998). This reality, coupled with high-stakes testing that is continually evolving faster than anybody can stay on top of, leads people to communicate in the style in which they are most comfortable.

Think of yourself for a moment and your preferred style of communication. I am predisposed to direct, blunt communication. I am aware that my style is not always effective for conveying the message that I want, but under stress or in times of urgency, I revert back to it. Teachers are the same way. For teachers, this might not mean using blunt and direct speech as in my case, but it may mean that when a unit is running long, you resort back to your preferred, easier instructional methodology of displaying notes on an overhead, irrespective of how students typically respond to that instructional style. In essence, communication just happens and is often unintentional. Daily stressors, including the massive amount of material to cover, can cause our decision-making and communication to become reactionary or driven by personal comfort. What gets lost is an opportunity to communicate for the learners and best support their learning process.

Example of Excellence

My favorite teacher from whom I had the pleasure of learning is Mr. Colin Hopper. I have written many essays about Mr. Hopper and am happy to have told him to his face that he was the best teacher I ever had. But like many students, I did not understand why he was my favorite until much later in life. I had the benefit of years of schooling about education to promote my understanding of what made him so outstanding. It is my honor to share a little story about Mr. Hopper that demonstrates his excellence in communicating for his students, not to them.

Mr. Hopper was a historian's historian. He loved charts, graphs, and maps, and could mesmerize his class with personal stories and then relate them to the most intricate historical scenarios. During a unit on the Civil War, Mr. Hopper's objective was for students to evaluate the circumstances of a battle and decipher if factors other than army size or weaponry could be important. Mr. Hopper began the lesson, and it quickly became clear that the class, me included, was struggling with the abstract concept. At that time, instead of continuing through the material—which might have been tempting since this was a Unites States history course with plenty to get through—he stopped the lesson and brought a friend and me to the side of the room. He asked if we would take part in a demonstration that involved him throwing stuff at us for fun. Being 16, we thought this sounded really fun, and of course we obliged.

Mr. Hopper stationed us at the back of the classroom. Our instructions were clear: When he said "Go," we were to charge at him and throw racquetballs at him. The rest of the class sat anxiously to see what was about to unfold. Mr. Hopper yelled "Go," and then he jumped on top of his desk and began pelting us with racquetballs as we attempted to throw ours at him. Our thirty-foot trek across the room took us about 20 seconds. In addition, his place on the desk and the fact that we were being pelted with racquetballs made it nearly impossible to remove him from his position. After a few minutes, Mr. Hopper yelled "Stop," and we returned to our desks.

Mr. Hopper then explained to the class that although he was outnumbered and battled two students larger than him, he dominated that fight for one main reason. He paused, and at that moment he taught us something that I would wager many of us have never forgotten. When it comes to battle, elevation can be every bit as important as numbers or weaponry.

This was by no means Mr. Hopper's preferred communication style, but in this case I do not believe that there could have been a more effective way to communicate the lesson.

Why This Is a Learner-Centered Strategy

Mr. Hopper adapted his personal communication style to meet the needs of his students. He may have taught that lesson five times that day and only had to act it out for our class. He may teach the same lesson today by showing a video, playing a podcast, or posting to a blog. The reason this is a learner-centered strategy is that although the outcome (what students must learn as a result of the lesson) was rigid, the methodology used to promote mastery of the outcome was completely based on the needs of the students in the class at that time. The teacher responded to feedback, adjusted the plan of attack, and did not settle until students could demonstrate understanding of the essential concept.

Elements of Learner-Centered Communication

While the Mr. Hopper story is an Example of Excellence, it is not intended to be an all-inclusive example or even to be modeled. There are many things that can transform daily communication in a classroom into a learner-centered experience that promotes a positive atmosphere and increased learning. Learner-centered communication should include the following components:

- Clearly-stated outcomes
- Responsiveness to student needs
- Diverse methodologies
- Multiple modalities
- The infusion of technology when appropriate

Clearly-Stated Outcomes

Every lesson should have one component that is rigid and unyielding—the desired outcome. All lessons are different, but they all need a guide for student learning. Highly-effective lessons, at one point or another, have the intended outcome clearly stated, written, and checked for understanding. The traditional format for this is as follows: the objective is written on the board and articulated at the beginning of class, and some type of check for understanding takes place at the end of class or before independent practice. While this may be the traditional methodology, some lessons are more impactful if the learning target is not conveyed until the end of a lesson or activity. This is fine, as long as in every lesson, the clearly stated outcome is directly communicated to students.

Here are some quick reminders and suggestions relating to communicating outcomes:

◆ The outcome must be addressed three times—once in writing, once verbally, and once through a check for understanding.
◆ The outcome should be stated in a format that could easily transfer to an assessment question. For instance, "today we will learn about frogs" is not an outcome statement. An outcome statement is "As a result of this lesson, students will be able to compare the anatomy of a frog and toad."
◆ I encourage teachers struggling through this process to think of a teacher-created study guide. If students were to copy the outcome statements of each lesson into their notebooks (highly suggested), would it look like a study guide? If so, you have accomplished your goal. Writing outcome statements like this does two things for teachers. First, it allows students to understand how they will be assessed. Second, it clearly communicates the learning expectations for kids.

Responsiveness to Student Needs

Being reactionary is seldom discussed as a positive trait for teachers. However, being in tune with your students and reacting to their needs is a great way to communicate in a learner-centered manner. This is something I struggled with as a teacher, as many people do. When one of my students struggled with a concept, I first repeated it slower. If slower did not work, I tried louder. If that did not work, I combined the two into a very loud, very slow explanation of the content. These strategies did not produce the increases in learning that I desired. Below, we've outlined a prescriptive and more effective manner for being reactive. This process helps teachers plan how to be reactive (so it doesn't become something stressful you have to do on the spot), while remaining learner centered.

1. Elicit feedback multiple times each day.
   a. It is impossible to react to something that you do not know exists. As a teacher, imagine yourself as a salesperson trying to

win an account. It would be ineffective to plow through a 45-minute slideshow and then simply ask at the end if the person wants to buy the product. As a salesman, you would gauge body language, ask questions throughout, and maintain a constant sense of the "temperature" of the room. If things were going well, you would continue; if they were not, you would adjust on the fly and do whatever you could to get everybody back on board. As a teacher, it should be no different, except you're not selling a product; you're selling the content and skills deemed essential. A teacher can garner feedback in a variety of ways:

   i.   Body language

   ii. Voluntary participation

   iii. Checks for understanding

   iv. Responses to questions

2. Use students.

   a. Once feedback is garnered that some of the class is not making the desired progress toward a specific outcome, it is important to see if the lack of progress is the norm for the classroom. A technique to use when this occurs is the simple, "Ask three before you ask me." This sentiment from a teacher to students allows students to work together and allows for many different instructional strategies to be used simultaneously throughout the classroom by many different "mini-teachers."

3. Elicit feedback.

   a. If feedback is positive and the concepts and material are understood, the lesson can progress. Before the lesson progresses, great teachers use this as an opportunity to continue to adapt and improve upon their craft. A question such as, "Those of you who struggled getting it when I was presenting—what did your classmates do that I can do next time to make the lesson better?" Not only does this question allow you to get additional input, but it also forces students to explain their methodology, thus reinforcing the concept internally and exposing the remainder of the students to that technique.

   b. If the feedback is negative, this is where a teacher can be forced to adapt the lesson quickly and try to reach students in a different manner. This is where being proactive about being reactive truly helps the effectiveness of a teacher. When planning, a teacher who has methods a, b, and c to deliver a lesson will be at a decided advantage over a teacher who is only prepared to deliver the material in one way.

4. Repeat the above cycle.

Diverse Methodologies

Classroom routines can be a positive thing, but using the same pedagogy for all content is not an effective teaching practice. Sticking with the same unit plan calling for a PowerPoint at the same point each day, requiring group work at the same time, and distributing quizzes on the same day each week exists for one reason: the preference of the teacher. Changing this practice to match the needs of the students will be a gigantic change in practice for some, but one that is necessary if a classroom is going to be learner-centered. Remember the often quoted definition of insanity: doing the same thing and expecting a different response. If you give a PowerPoint every day, followed by independent practice, followed by a quiz on Tuesday, and the majority of students are getting Cs, Ds, and Fs, this grade trajectory will continue unless you change.

Truly learner-centered teachers are constantly adapting their professional practice and detailing their success. They don't do this by randomly changing practice. They become excellent by taking data and gaining an understanding of when they are at their most effective (measured by student learning) for a given set of students.

Multiple Modalities

If something is important to your class, it needs to be communicated multiple times in multiple ways. Simply stating it once does not adequately communicate the message. Placing the message on the board, saying it out loud, placing it on the assignment or coursework for the day, *and* posting it on a classroom Facebook page does. Following are some ideas for communicating important messages, besides in the typical verbal manner. Using a variety of these methods will make your message more learner-centered.

- ◆ The teacher writes it on the board.
- ◆ Students write it in their notebooks.
- ◆ The teacher writes it on the assessment.
- ◆ Students repeat it chorally as a group.
- ◆ The teacher posts it on Facebook.
- ◆ The teacher tweets it.
- ◆ The teacher represents it visually without words or numbers.

The goal of teaching is to have ALL students learn. Quite often, communication will have to take place a number of times in different manners in order to reach all students.

The Infusion of Technology When Appropriate

The classroom of 2020 should not look like the classroom of 2010 if the intended outcome of public education is to prepare students for success in the outside world. To prepare students for life in the 21st century, we must teach like we are in the 21st century. This means that practice must change in kindergarten through high school to become learner-centered and to meet the ever-changing needs of students. This extends beyond the simple inclusion of technology, or even beyond a school going to a one-to-one (student to computer) ratio. This means changing practices to use technology to enhance instruction and thus student learning. As educators, we should believe that the message we are trying to communicate to students is of the utmost importance. If that is our true belief, then it becomes our responsibility to get that message across to students in any manner possible. Here are three methods of communication, facilitated by the Internet, that every teacher should become familiar with and begin using:

- ◆ **Blogs**. In my experience, some educators can be resistant to technology—especially to the incorporation of technology in the primary grades. But in my opinion, there is no reason that blogging should not begin in the third grade. In fact, my experience indicates that blogs can be effective even earlier. Blogs have many educational uses and benefits, but in terms of learner-centered communication, they allow teachers to facilitate a conversation around a central theme or issue. This allows for students to have their voices heard and to hear the voices of their peers in an organized, non-threatening manner that not only promotes mastery of the objective but also promotes writing skills and the use of technology.
- ◆ **Social media**. Kids use Facebook, tweet, watch YouTube, send Instagrams, use Tumblr, and pin on Pinterest. If we know that our students use those tools, then we need to meet them there with our message. Some proactive teachers establish websites to be used as electronic course guides. However, that is telling kids to leave the sites they already visit to do something explicitly for school. If we go to where they are at, we become learner centered in intent.
- ◆ **Pre-constructed lesson briefs**. As teachers, you don't always have to reinvent the wheel. More and more websites, such as TedEd, Khan Academy, and YouTube, are beginning to post pre-recorded lesson briefs. While I do not believe that these briefs are as valuable as a classroom teacher, I do believe that they provide diversity of message and can be used to enhance nearly any lesson with a corresponding desired outcome. Additionally, these briefs are not only for outside entities to complete. Podcasts and video recordings of lessons are extremely valuable and speak directly to learner-centered communication. The value in having a repeat of a lesson one-click away or having the original lesson one-click away for somebody who was absent demonstrates exactly what the paradigm shift from adult- or content-centered education to learner-centered education is all about.

Provide a Roadmap

Imagine that you are in the lobby of a 5-star hotel located on the Gulf Coast of Florida. The expansive resort has more than 1,350 rooms, multiple conference centers, six pools, four restaurants, and of course a sprawling beach. Your challenge is to blindfold whomever you are with—husband, wife, son, daughter, friend, or colleague—and with the help of a map and the hotel's signage, use only words to lead your partner to your room from the lobby and then from the room to the beach. This task may be tricky, and at times you may need to redo some steps, but most partners will end up on the beach.

So, how is this scenario analogous to education? In the scenario, the leader (teacher) must guide his or her partner (student) to the desired outcome (the beach). But even if the person was able to traverse the hotel to get to the desired outcome, is it repeatable? Does the person know the value of what he or she just did, or why he or she was able to do certain things at certain times? In the increasingly high-stakes world of education, we become so focused on getting students from Point A to Point B that ensuring that students understand the *purpose and process* to a desired outcome becomes a secondary or tertiary objective. This is not the case in a learner-centered classroom.

The Common Reality

As students progress through the compulsory schooling experience, some-how the curiosity that they had in the elementary grades gets lost by the time they enter high school. Having children at home reinforces this obser-vation. Spend a day with five-year-olds and chart how many questions they ask you. Then do the same with 15-year-olds and notice the differ-ence. Somehow, the ability or willingness to express curiosity wanes.

Instead of noticing this change and working to re-engage students in their education, we allow this diminished curiosity to impact instruction. We no longer feel compelled to focus on purpose and process within the classroom since it is not demanded of us by our students. Students become passengers in cars traveling from point to point instead of becoming their own personal navigators and masters of their own journey. Fortunately, we have the power and ability to change this by adapting a handful of our current instructional practices and creating a learner-centered environ-ment within the classroom.

 Example of Excellence

Most of you reading this book already have some great instructional meth-ods in your arsenal. Our intention in providing guidance and examples is to help you reflect and find ways to adapt and continually improve. It is important that the focus remain on adapting a strategy in light of new thoughts and reflection, not on quickly adopting something you read in a journal article or book or heard at a conference. Adaptation calls for a com-mitment to sustaining pieces of practice that were effective and replacing the ones that were not. It is not a total abandonment of the current practice. Keep that in mind when considering the following Example of Excellence.

Students walked into Mr. Zielinski's sixth-grade class on the first day of a new unit, ready for an event they have grown accustomed to: pre-assessment day. Before Mr. Zielinski's class, students had not been exposed to pre-assessment in the manner in which he uses it, so he was met with some resistance at first. Once students realized that pre-assessments could not hurt their grades and helped Mr. Zielinski know what not to teach, they embraced them.

After a 20-minute pre-assessment was over, Mr. Zielinski collected the work and asked them to recall what the questions on the pre-assessment were asking. The students articulated the questions, and Mr. Zielinski wrote them on the board. The students corrected the minor errors, and after about ten minutes the students were able to get near- perfect recitations of each of the four open-ended questions asked about the Civil War. Mr. Zie-linski then asked if the students could tell him why those questions were asked, to which a choral response echoed in the room, "Because those are the things we need to be able to know and do to be successful in this unit." This choral response prompted another question from Mr. Z, as he was affectionately known, asking what students' next step should be. To this they responded, "Copy down the information on the board."

The students were given a few moments to accomplish this task. Afterward, Mr. Zielinski went to the board and told students to prepare for "WWH." Students reached into their belongings, pulled out their notebooks, and began to create a table containing the outcome for the day (as it was written on the board) and three rows labeled *What*, *Why*, and *How*. The outcome for the first lesson of the unit was for students to create a list of things they found valuable enough to risk their life or lifestyle for and then write an essay explaining why. The students copied down the objective, and then the class began a discussion of WHAT (the first *W*) that would look like on an assignment, WHY (the second *W*) that may be a desired outcome (in light of what they already know about the unit) and HOW (the *H*) they think this may facilitate further learning in the future.

Students completed this chart in thinking groups, and then the full class engaged in a discussion around those questions, culminating in the daily activity he called the five WHY's. Students had the opportunity to ask the teacher five "Why" questions regarding the outcome or outcomes, but the questions had to be somehow tied to school and what they were learning. If a student asked a question Mr. Z could not answer, the student received a small incentive like a pen, pencil, or piece of candy. This process took Mr. Z a bit of time to norm each year, but by October, students knew the routine. The kinds of questions he received included, "Why does this relate to the Civil War?" or "Why are we going to write an essay about something personal when we are going to learn about something that happened hundreds of years ago?" Once the questioning was over, students began a discussion focused on the topic at hand for the day and the expectations on their assignment.

Why This Is a Learner-Centered Strategy

Each segment of Mr. Zielinski's lesson focused on two things: the students and the desired outcome. The very first thing he did to introduce the unit (the pre-assessment) allowed students to view desired outcomes and to measure their current level of knowledge and skill against the desired outcome. The next activities (copying the pre-assessment questions and completing WWH) forced kids to keep a record of, and actively think about, desired outcomes. This process personalized the outcome before content was even discussed or considered. The last teacher-led activity—the five why's—created student interaction, provided purpose to the desired outcome(s), and rewarded inquisitiveness.

Elements of Learner-Centered Outcome Creation and Communication

Mr. Zielinski certainly had an excellent, very learner-centered and outcome-driven lesson, but is it possible to replicate that on a daily basis? The answer is the exceedingly non-descript: sort of. Every teacher should strive to have every lesson of every chapter of every unit be excellent and learner-centered, but the reality is that not every lesson will reach that critical benchmark. In order to ensure the best possible performance, how-ever, several components of learner-centered and outcome-driven activi-ties should be incorporated into all unit and lesson planning sessions:

♦ Pre-assessments
♦ Daily what, why, and how
♦ Five whys of outcome statements
♦ Student-designed study guides

Pre-Assessments

To be learner-centered, the teacher paradigm for giving a pre-assessment should be to procure *and* to disseminate valuable information. During pre-assessment, teachers should collect information to determine the read-iness level of all students in comparison to the desired outcomes, and students should collect information as to the knowledge and skills they must acquire to be successful in a given unit. Pre-assessment should not only impact how teachers instruct but also impact how students learn. Pre-assessment best practices include these:

♦ Align tasks directly with desired outcomes and with
   post-assessment.
♦ Create content-rich but skill-based questions.
♦ Do an assessment recap.
♦ Use the results to inform instruction.

Align Tasks Directly with Desired Outcomes and with Post-Assessment
Outcomes and pre- and post-assessments need to be directly aligned in order to maximize effectiveness. I have always found it beneficial to exam-ine this process visually (see Figure 3.1, page 23). Using this visual, linear model helps teachers to abandon that one favorite lesson that does not directly apply to the desired objectives of a unit and does not further stu-dent skill and knowledge development to support their success on a sum-mative assessment.

Create Content-Rich But Skill-Based Questions
Working on constructing quality pre-assessments can often alert teachers to deficiencies in their graded assessments. For instance, consider this question:

Figure 3.1 Aligning Pre- and Post-Assessments

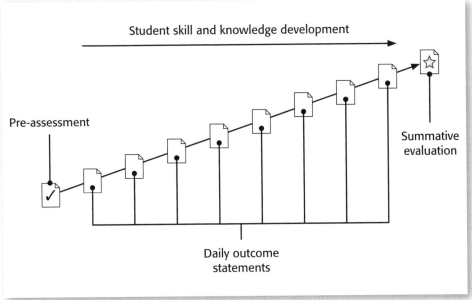

Around what time did the American Civil War begin?
a) 1750   b) 1800
b) 1850   d) 1900

That question requires pure memorization, and if it is asked on the pre-assessment, it essentially gives students one free question. Teachers often shy away from pre-assessment because they view it as a "giveaway" or a practice that actually decreases student learning. The thought is this: *If I ask about the date of an event on the pre-assessment and students know that it will show up on the summative assessment, all they need to do is memorize it in order to get the question right.* But the issue is not the pre-assessment, it is the question. Consider the content-rich, skill-based question that could have been asked instead:

◆ *How did the time period of the Civil War impact the potential outcome of the war?* This pre-assessment question requires student to know when the war began, plus use critical thinking skills to understand the implications that a time period plays on the course of war.

A similar question that requires the same knowledge and skill base could easily be asked on a post-assessment:

◆ *Compare and contrast the Civil War with what would happen if states tried to secede in the present day.*

This process not only provides information for both the student and the teacher, but also helps provide a system for vetting assessment questions and increasing rigor in the course.

Do an Assessment Recap

Learner-centered teachers force students to think about everything that takes place in the classroom. Asking students questions that they have already been given the answer to or that have no right answers provides a safe environment for everybody to get involved. After a pre-assessment, the students and teacher should discuss the questions that were asked— starting with simply identifying the questions asked. Once that is achieved, facilitate student learning by having students think about why those questions would be asked on a pre-assessment and what their guess is as to the purpose of a particular question. This mirrors a process many teachers have participated in called "unwrapping the standard." Can students unwrap a question to understand what it truly means? This process not only encourages student dialogue about future outcomes but also allows students to focus on what has been deemed essential for them to learn throughout the unit.

Use the Results to Inform Instruction

Lastly, and quite possibly most importantly, pre-assessment must inform instruction on multiple levels. After reviewing the data from pre-assessments, the teacher must decide which outcomes are already mastered by the class and do not need to be focused on, and which students need enrichment on certain elements of a unit because they show a level of personal mastery. Great teachers never neglect to collect and analyze data to make such decisions. Doing so is essential to transform your classroom into a learner-centered environment.

Daily What, Why, and How

Think back to the analogy at the beginning of the chapter about blindly guiding somebody to a destination as opposed to creating a roadmap. With a roadmap, and the skills to decipher it, somebody can return to the desired location many times from many different starting points and always be successful. The Daily What, Why, How (WWH) is a lesson-based roadmap to learning.

The teaching process includes simply introducing the WWH graphic organizer, introducing the outcome on a daily basis, and then facilitating discussion. An example of the graphic organizer is shown in Figure 3.2 (page 25).

The purpose of asking "what" is to have students take the "education-ese" from the outcome statement and put the learning target into their own words. This not only personalizes the learning but also requires students

Figure 3.2 WWH Graphic Organizer

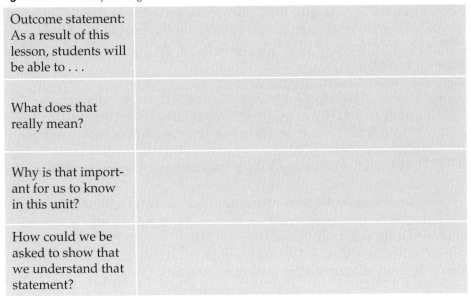

Outcome statement: As a result of this lesson, students will be able to . . .	
What does that really mean?	
Why is that important for us to know in this unit?	
How could we be asked to show that we understand that statement?	

to hone in on what they are to be thinking about the remainder of the class. Asking "why" requires students to provide relevance to their own learning. It also provides students the opportunity to link the current lesson outcome to things learned previously. The "how" urges students to consider how this might be assessed. This strategy not only creates an outcome-based culture in the classroom but also prompts students to learn items in depth. When students gain practice thinking like a teacher and wondering how a certain topic or outcome statement will look when it appears on an assessment, it will force them to use critical thinking skills and thus deepen their learning.

Five Whys of Outcome Statements

Examine the inquiry level in a ninth-grade classroom compared to a fifth-grade classroom compared to a first-grade classroom, and you'll see a decreasing level of student inquiry. People with young children can tell you that they cannot count on ten hands the number of times a day that they are asked "Why," "What if," or "How." On the other hand, anybody with teenagers can tell you that the incidents of them asking a question and possibly extending a conversation with their parents are few and far between. What happens to the natural inquisitiveness of kids, and how can we facilitate its continuance? The answer is simple: provide incentives and make it a priority.

Every day, students should be encouraged to quiz the teacher on why what they are learning is important. For learning to be student-centered, students must know the purpose of the activities they are asked to complete. By allotting two minutes daily for students to dig deeper into why they must learn something, teachers empower the learners and help them realize the relevancy of the topic. Here is the process for the Five Whys lesson segment:

- ◆ Students have two minutes at the conclusion of introductory activities (WWH) to ask their teacher up to five questions beginning with the word *Why* that concern the daily outcome and are school or course related.
- ◆ If the teacher cannot answer a question, the student receives an incentive (candy, pen, pencil, sticker).
- ◆ The system must become routine–preferably repeated daily.

Student-Designed Study Guides

There are generally three schools of thought when it comes to study guides.

1. Give students everything—provide as many questions and cues as possible so that students know what to study and can master essential content. If students complete the guide with fidelity, they should do very well on the assessment.
2. Give them some stuff—provide enough material to steer student studying. If students complete the guide with fidelity, they should certainly not fail the assessment.
3. Give them nothing—provide no additional material to students. The thought is that this teaches students responsibility since they are in charge of their own learning.

As you may have already discerned, we listed these philosophies regarding study guides in terms of their level of being student-centered, with number one being the most and number three being the least. The ideal practice is a combination of number one and number three. If a teacher follows the practices listed throughout this chapter, there may be no need to ever "create" a study guide again, and students will still be thoroughly informed of everything they are expected to know and be able to do. Using the table format for daily WWH as explained previously, students, on a daily basis, write down the intended outcome as well as why it is important and how they may be assessed on that item. At the conclusion of a unit, that table is now a complete study guide for students. More importantly, teachers have provided a detailed roadmap, which will allow students to find their own paths to success.

Give the Work Back

Many different educators have attempted to articulate the concept of giving back the work to students. The most frequently-used analogy to convey this message is often attributed to William Butler Yeats: "Education is not the filling of a pail, but the lighting of a fire." The concept is that education and learning should no longer be thought of as a passive process in which the learner simply receives information from a teacher. We cannot simply crack open students' skulls and pour information into their brains. Instead, we must work as facilitators or guides through the process, so that students can truly master and use the information being taught and not just learn it for a singular, fleeting moment.

Every parent of a child six years old or older has gone through the process of trying to teach that child how to tie his or her shoes. I know no experience quite like my own, so I will share with you the error of my ways and how I grew as an educator from the experience.

About eight months before my oldest son was to start kindergarten, I reached out to a local kindergarten teacher and asked for her set of learning outcomes for students. She obliged, and within a matter of moments I was holding a list of several things that I could work on with my son over the next few months—one being tying his shoes. Tying shoes, for whatever reason, stuck out to me and became an area of focus for the next few weeks. We discussed the two "best practice" methods of rabbit ear versus loop, swoop, pull, but we still were running into difficulty. Then, perplexed by the delay in improvement, I discovered that teaching him how to tie a bow on the drawstring of athletic shorts seemed to be much easier. Within a week, he just about had it down.

As life became busy—as it always does—shoe tying became less of a priority. In fact, our efforts devolved into me simply repeating loop, swoop, and pull as I hurriedly put on his sneakers each morning and we ran off to start the day. For the next six months, my son watched me tie his shoes and could label each action that I completed—loop, swoop, pull. As June became July and then quickly August, I thought it was time to start practicing this process again. Six months later—with the steps loop, swoop, and pull firmly memorized, my son had actually regressed in terms of being able to tie his shoes. He regressed because as things became busy, I did the work for him, and he was unable to practice mastering the skill.

The Common Reality

Teachers work hard. In fact, I cannot think of a nobler, harder-working set of individuals in any profession that does not involve literally putting your life on the line. My wife is a teacher—and a good one. She spends time nightly reflecting on her practice and truly cares about her students. By no stretch of the imagination does she ever work a forty-hour work week, nor are her summers "off." Teaching can be a grind and take its toll on a professional. If you don't believe me, take an impromptu photo of your staff at the November or February staff meeting and compare that to the ID picture taken at the beginning of the year. Most of the staff will look tired, pale, and as if they need a hug!

This chapter is designed to allow teachers to give themselves a virtual hug by abandoning their responsibility for some of the tedious, time-consuming tasks that they arduously complete week after week. Learning to let go of some of the tasks that you know harm your practice in order to concentrate on higher-yield initiatives will elevate your performance from good to great and raise you to a truly distinguished level.

Example of Excellence

Stacy Spratt is a first-grade teacher at Learning Gifted Academy (LGA) in Minneapolis, Minnesota. Stacy has taught at LGA for three years and has established a wonderful reputation among her colleagues and throughout the community. The learner-centered lesson described here revolved around a mid-unit formative assessment.

During the second half of math instruction on Tuesday, Ms. Spratt had students separate into four groups to work on assessment preparation. The learning outcomes for the unit were:

1. Partition circles and rectangles into two and four equal shares.
2. Describe the shares using the words *halves, fourths,* and *quarters,* and use the phrases *half of, fourth of,* and *quarter of.*
3. Describe the whole as two of, or four of the shares.
4. Understand for these examples that decomposing into more equal shares creates smaller shares.

Each outcome statement was assigned to a table. As students rotated from table to table, their charge was to create one easy, one medium, and one hard question and provide the answer. Student groups had five to ten minutes to work at each table and create questions. Once the questions were created, they were deposited into a box on each table.

Ms. Spratt then evaluated the questions submitted and organized an assessment for the following day that was separated by the four outcome statements listed above. Students were given the assessment at the outset of the next lesson and were given time to complete it. Upon completion of the assessment, students were instructed to take out a grading implement and self-evaluate their work. Ms. Spratt provided a detailed explanation of each question and answer, and students marked up their own work.

Students were then asked to complete a reflection statement. Given that this lesson took place in spring, students were well-versed in this process. Students were to pick the outcome statement listed above that they needed the most help with—based upon their data and using their own thinking to break a tie. Students then created a document that looked like Figure 4.1 (page 30).

Then Ms. Spratt had *every* student come to the board to place a mark next to the outcome that he or she needed the most help with. Since all students—even the high-achievers—were required to identify areas of improvement, this activity did not single anybody out or cause stress for students.

After compiling that information, Ms. Spratt indicated that it looked as if the class needed the most help with describing the whole as two of, or four of the shares. Ms. Spratt said that not everybody mentioned that they needed help in this area and asked if anybody had ideas on how she could teach the material differently or better. Several students raised their hand and described how they learned the material on their own or with the help of their parents. After listening to the students' explanations, Ms. Spratt wrapped up the math lesson for the day. At the conclusion of the lesson, Ms. Spratt accessed her professional Facebook page and quickly typed: "The practice test [not all parents understand "formative assessment"] showed that our class needs more help studying describing the whole as

Figure 4.1 Student Data and Reflection Statements

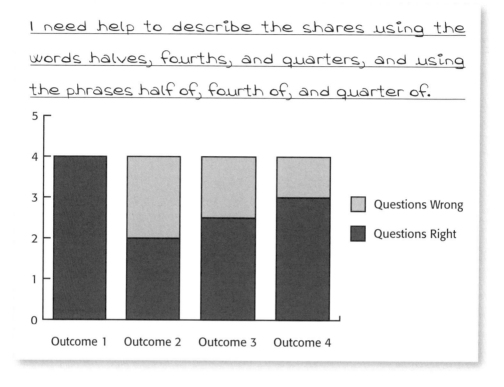

I need help to describe the shares using the words halves, fourths, and quarters, and using the phrases half of, fourth of, and quarter of.

two of, or four of the shares (as described in the handout sent home earlier in the week). Please review this topic with your children if the opportunity for practice exists at home."

Why This Is a Learner-Centered Strategy

Students were involved in every possible aspect of this lesson and assessment. First, they were allowed to take part in the creation of the assessment (while reviewing the material). Next, they corrected their own work so they could compare exactly what they did with how the teacher described they should have done the work. In addition, this was a formative assessment, so students were not tempted to hide their mistakes or be inaccurate in order to improve their grade. Each step of the process was results-neutral. Students then completed their own feedback forms, analyzed their own data, and created a classroom data breakdown on their own. After an area for growth was identified, the teacher allowed the students to propose potential solutions or explanations for other students to listen to and possibly adopt. This also allowed the teacher to gain a better understanding of which students could be utilized to support the learning of others and/or which students would benefit from enrichment work on this particular outcome.

Elements of Giving the Work Back

Teacher effort does not equate to teacher effectiveness. You must adopt that philosophy in order to make the conscious effort to give the work back to the students. Doing so will not only promote some best practice methodologies that might otherwise be missing from your repertoire, but it will also more actively engage students in the learning process. Here are five aspects of giving the work back:

- ◆ Monitored airtime
- ◆ Student creation of assessment/assessment review
- ◆ Student-work portfolios
- ◆ Student-led identification of areas to be retaught
- ◆ Student-led communication with home

Monitored Airtime

Imagine a classroom where the teacher is at the front of the room giving a well-prepared lecture. What is happening when a classroom is dominated by the voice of the teacher? Kids may be learning, but they are learning because they are making a choice to interact with the teacher and the content. Think of it this way—we can passively watch cooking shows for hours on end and become a marginally more informed and better cook. Think of the difference, however, if we went to cooking class where we were taught and then interacted with the material. We would become substantially better using this latter method. In the same way, we can create lessons and environments that substantially promote the interaction of students with the material. These lessons do not involve much teacher talking. These lessons are created by teachers who do not view students as buckets into which information can be poured. Instead, these lessons are focused on the students and are creatively designed to foster active learning and interaction with the material.

While monitoring your own airtime may seem like a simple concept, it is easier to implement if you keep in mind these three things:

- ◆ **Impose a five-minute limit**. Certain lessons call for direct instruction. Teachers must take time to teach the content; that is understood. Just teach the lesson in chunks of no more than five minutes. It is almost impossible to envision a lesson that could not benefit from limiting the duration of teacher-only talking to five minute chunks.
- ◆ **Script questions**. Teachers talk more in order to ensure that students learn what is desired. Think of a time when you adopted the mindset, "There is an objective to this lesson, and darn it, I am going to make sure that I get the kids there—and TODAY!" The

best teachers can get to the same end point by asking a series of well-constructed, open-ended, conversation-starting questions. Some teachers have a natural talent for doing so. If this does not come naturally to you, you may wish to begin by scripting questions.

◆ **Don't require direct note taking**. Extinguish the practice of direct note taking in which the teacher stands at the board, overhead, Elmo, or LCD projector and simply dictates the notes as students copy them. This is the exact definition of teacher- and content-centered instruction. There is no circumstance in which this practice is the best methodology for students to learn material.

Student Creation of Assessment/Assessment Review

I distinctly remember sitting with my friends in high school trying to figure out what to study for a test. Imagine that—high school kids sitting around, wanting to do well, wanting to study, and being forced to page through 70 pages of a European history text guessing what the teacher found important in that chapter. Great teachers do not allow this to happen. Great teachers not only make sure that students know what to study but also involve students in the process.

Note: Before we get into the details of this practice, it is important that you identify whether your students should contribute to assessment review or assessment creation in your particular circumstance. Many schools have adopted common formative and summative assessments, and thus the practice of allowing students to help create assessment contradicts a current building- or district-supported practice and should not occur. In those situations, teachers should focus on having students help create assessment reviews that will direct student efforts during studying.

The process of student-supported assessment creation or review accomplishes four very important things when done appropriately.

1. It forces students to think about what they were supposed to have learned.
2. It makes students imagine how they could be assessed.
3. It has students work to create answers to potential questions.
4. It broadens students' understanding of rigor and critical-thinking skills.

Teachers can ensure those four things occur by following these guiding principles: Students are to work in small groups, create questions that support and align with essential learning outcomes, provide answers to the questions they created, and create questions with intentionally different levels of rigor. This process saves teachers the sometimes very time-consuming process of creating review activities and actively engages students in learning, reflection, and cooperative effort.

Student Work Portfolios

Almost every adult I know has been on a diet at some point in his or her life. When dieting, people weigh themselves. Some do it every day, others do it three times a week, and others do it twice a month or less frequently. The reason for weighing ourselves is quite simple: It allows us to track our progress, which provides motivation either through positive or negative results, and it allows ownership of the behaviors that helped produce the results. If we know that tracking progress in an autonomous fashion can help improve results, then it only makes sense to create a way to do that with student progress.

Moreover, the teacher has long been viewed as someone who is the "keeper of the grades." How many times have students or parents said, "Mrs. Smith *gave* me a D?" I have heard comments like that throughout my career. Student work portfolios allow teachers to quickly demonstrate to students or parents why students received the grades that they did. It transfers ownership of student progress, and therefore grading, from the teacher to the student. To maximize the effectiveness of student portfolios, five things need to occur.

1. Students need to be responsible for the creation/maintenance of the portfolio.
   - This process is designed to take work from the teacher, not create additional work.
   - Creating a system of assessment or assignment return and student reflection on their progress should not be too time-consuming, since benchmarking does not happen that often.
2. Portfolios must be kept in the teacher's room or saved electronically.
   - For portfolios to be meaningful, they must track progress over time. Thus, keeping the material safe and accessible is extremely important.
   - Electronic portfolios are safer, easier to monitor, and lend themselves to better organization.
3. Portfolios should be organized by progress toward a specified outcome.
   - Organize the materials in a portfolio by outcomes, not by chronological order.
4. Students' reflections on their performance toward each outcome should be documented after posted assignments.
   - Without this component, portfolios may be nothing more than comprehensive folders.

5. Portfolios must follow students from year-to-year and teacher-to-teacher.
    *   This process demonstrates alignment of courses by outcome and allows for reflection upon growth at multiple levels.

Student-Led Identification of Areas to be Retaught

Collecting and analyzing data has become something that all great teachers must do. However, it cannot always be done as efficiently or effectively as teachers might like. Imagine that a short-answer, three-question "exit slip" version of formative assessment was given to tenth graders regarding the outcomes covered in chemistry for the past three days by their teacher, Mr. Morris. Given the typical use of exit slips as formative assessment, Mr. Morris would then have to correct 450 questions and break down data for six different sections of class before he could even begin to plan for instruction the next day. Since Mr. Morris is committed to best practice and the assessment results will impact his class preparation, he may have six similar, yet different, lesson plans to correct after the original data analysis is over.

The same three questions could be part of a formative assessment and then could be discussed in class, and students could articulate concerns over their progress toward an objective. By establishing a culture within the class that formative assessment is *for* learning, not to *grade* learning, students will be more willing to share their results and progress. Here is the strategy that I have found to be the most beneficial for collecting and analyzing data while maintaining confidentiality of student progress.

*   The teacher places the outcomes being assessed on the board and labels them A, B, C, etc.
*   The teacher informs students that they must assign (x) amount of points to the board, assigning more points to the areas in which they need more support. (x equals the total number of outcomes listed.)
    *   If a student feels he or she aced the assessment, then he or she must assign points—in that case it would be 1 to each area.
    *   If a student only struggled on outcome two, all three points would be assigned there.
    *   The teacher then instructs the students to shout out their answers as the teacher records them.
    *   Any outcome with a total more than 1.25 the number of students in the course needs to be retaught.

This process may take several minutes the first time you do it, but after a few weeks, it will take only a few moments. It is yet another way of communicating to students that the class is outcome-driven and that the teacher is responsive to student needs. It saves teachers time from pouring over simple data analysis and frees them up to do more intensive instructional, enrichment, and remediation planning.

Student-Led Communication with Home

Involving families in their child's education is without a doubt best practice. My experience has taught me that the perceived importance and necessity of this form of communication wanes each year a child progresses through school. Take, for example, my current district. I receive weekly bulletins sent home with my first-grade son that we collectively review as a family, whereas less than ten percent of high school students have parental representation at parent-teacher conferences. Knowing that trend, the question becomes this: How can a district work to make communicating with families the most efficient and effective that it possibly can?

The answer is to involve students at all grade levels in the communication. Picture a group of five-year-olds. Would they be more excited to show their parents a piece of paper their teacher handed them or something that they created? Now think about teenagers. Would they be more likely to encourage their parents to attend a conference at school if they had nothing to do with it or if they planned the conference? If we want to promote parental engagement in education, then we must actively involve the students in the school's attempts to communicate with home. This process breaks into three tiers depending on the students' ages.

Tier One: Kindergarten Through Second Grade
At this stage, parents are likely heavily engaged in the educational process. Students should take ownership of some of the communication. This can be done in many ways, but one way is to select students to be weekly helpers for the communication home. Examples include these:

- Students help type the newsletter home.
- Student examples of work are embedded in the newsletter or posted online.
- Student reactions/quotes to work done or things learned are embedded in the newsletter/website.

Tier Two: Third Through Sixth Grade
This is typically the age group when parent participation starts to noticeably decline. Attempting to keep parents involved during this stage is noble, but many times the teacher's time and dedication are met with futile results. The best method to involve parents in their student's educational process is to have the communication be led directly by the student. Examples include these:

◆ Send home student-created letters at the end of each week.
◆ Have students create a personal electronic blog or portfolio of classroom activity.
◆ Create a classroom website (Facebook, EdModo, etc.) updated by students detailing events of the class.

Tier Three: Seventh Through Twelfth Grade

This age level presents the biggest challenge to teachers trying to involve families. More than likely, the only parents who are actively involved are the ones who do not need to be. Thus, students must completely lead this process for it to be meaningful. Examples include these:

◆ Hold student-led Parent-Student-Teacher conferences.
◆ Use portfolios for student-led interaction.
◆ Have students write reflections on their progress toward desired outcomes and e-mail those reflections to parents from the students' e-mail accounts.
◆ Have students create classroom websites.

Differentiate Daily

Differentiation is not a new concept. Each summer, I work with a group of students who will be interviewing for their first teaching position that year. As we brainstorm and prepare for interview questions, the vast majority respond that they expect a question about differentiation. They are most likely correct. Differentiation is mentioned in almost all frameworks for teaching—irrespective of which educational pundit's framework your state or district has adopted. Differentiation is not an educational fad. Differentiation is best practice. Differentiation is hard! Differentiation is an instructional method in which many teachers have room for growth and need support along the way.

The Common Reality

A teacher's classroom is a mixture of anywhere between fifteen and thirty students of varying backgrounds, abilities, interests, and learning styles. The expectation is that the teacher is supposed to support each student's growth from where he or she is currently performing to a higher level of learning. This is an overwhelmingly daunting task.

My experience indicates that most good teachers have identified skills that each student should know and be able to do to be successful in a unit of study. As the unit progresses, the teacher identifies those students whom they believe may be struggling and makes legitimate efforts to try and move those students toward competency

Thus, the common reality is that differentiation generally consists of non-planned activities to remediate students toward a standard and seldom includes enrichment activities. What is more dangerous is that "differentiation" can also become synonymous with "intervention." That is fine as long as intervention does not become synonymous with "somebody else's problem now." Great teachers do not allow this to happen.

Example of Excellence

Mr. Jonathon Gaines is a seventh-grade pre-algebra teacher in the western suburbs of Lincoln, Nebraska. Mr. Gaines teaches in a school that has consistently average test scores—except for his class. Mr. Gaines follows the same routines throughout the year—the same routine for every unit and the same routine for almost every class period.

Each unit begins the same way, with a pre-test broken down by standard, with multiple questions of varying difficulties for each standard. In order to maximize time, this assessment is generally given right after the post-assessment for a prior unit. The data from the pre-test is used to place each student into a group for each standard: 1—Emerging, 2—Projects to meet standard, 3—Projects to exceed standard.

Students are given a notecard with this information on it, as Mr. Gaines does not share that information freely with the class. Each lesson starts the same way, with Mr. Gaines seeking feedback on the prior day's work and assignment. Once that is complete, Mr. Gaines provides no more than fifteen minutes of instruction covering all of the necessary material for the day. Once he is done, he puts anywhere from one to three questions on the board dealing with the content he has just covered. Students work on the material as Mr. Gaines circles the room to provide immediate feedback to the students on their performance. He signs off on some students' papers.

After approximately five minutes, Mr. Gaines asks the students whose papers he signed to move to the back of the room while everybody else proceeds to the front. Those students are then assigned problems to fit the A category. They are either clustered as a 1A, 2A, or 3A depending on how they performed on this outcome during the pre-assessment. Each category has a different subsection of practice problems. This allows for enrichment activities to take place seamlessly within the confines of the traditional daily lesson.

Mr. Gaines then tweaks his instruction and performs practice problems at the board for the group who did not "get signed off on" during the first portion of class. The cycle then naturally repeats itself with the grouping of 1B, 2B, and 3B. All remaining students (generally few) begin to get immediate attention from Mr. Gaines. In addition, since the class is designed in this format, there are generally some students clustered in the A section for the lesson who can support the students at the front of the room in their efforts to demonstrate understanding of the skill taught that day.

Why This Is a Learner-Centered Strategy

Mr. Gaines clearly puts in a great deal of extra work in order to provide students their best opportunity to grow. The differentiation is directly based on students' performance against standards or outcomes—and based on multiple measures thereof. His typical lesson involves enrichment in multiple formats as well. Not only are students who show proficiency given different subsets of problems, but they are often utilized later in the same lesson to provide tutoring and reteaching support to their peers.

Elements of a Differentiated Classroom

You might find it overwhelming to try the techniques used by Mr. Gaines. However, remember this: You don't have to implement these techniques in the exact same way to become an effective differentiator in your class. However, you can learn from the key elements of Mr. Gaines' lesson. In particular, you should focus on these four key areas as you continue to develop the skill of differentiating:

♦ Multiple assessments of student progress
♦ Enrichment activities
♦ Remediation activities aligned to the stated outcome
♦ Preplanned activities.

Multiple Assessments of Student Progress

To differentiate instruction for a student and have it be meaningful, you must know precisely where the achievement level of the student is in comparison to the standard. In order to do so in a manner that best supports student learning, consider multiple measures. The rationale is that only accepting one measure provides an increased possibility that the measure was wrong. Consider the following scenarios (a few of the possible many) that could skew either a pre-assessment or daily formative assessment:

- ◆ Student had a bad day.
- ◆ Student was burned out after completing post-assessment.
- ◆ Student knew or understood skill, but needed refresher in order to show proficiency.
- ◆ Student had good luck on a single assessment.
- ◆ Assessment was poorly written or aligned.

Thus, multiple measures are necessary. The best way to go about this is a unit pre-assessment and daily formative assessment. The combined results should be able to prompt the teacher to react in a manner that truly blends the needs of the learner with the content to create a meaningful learning experience.

Pre-Assessment

Pre-assessment has already been discussed at length in this book. Its purpose is simple. To transition from a mindset in which your focus is the content, curriculum, and lesson plans to a mindset where your focus revolves around students, you must have a constant pulse on student progress toward proficiency of stated goals. The only way to do that effectively is to measure the temperature of students before instruction begins. Assuming students do not know what we think we need to teach them is not student centered.

As principal of a high school in a K–12 district, I was fortunate enough to have an art teacher who created a niche in the digital media curriculum for students to design posters supporting school improvement goals. One year early in my tenure, one of our goals was to complete curriculum mapping so that we could eliminate gaps and redundancies. A student created a propaganda poster for curriculum alignment stating, "If our curriculum is aligned, we will not have to learn about World War I for the fourth time." While the poster was funny, what it indicated about how kids were being educated was not. To be student-centered, we cannot assume student strengths and weaknesses. In addition, once we learn general strengths and weaknesses of students, we must be cautious to not assume student stagnation as the year progresses.

The first step to differentiation is simple: pre-assessment for every unit of every year—period.

Daily Formative Assessment

Every lesson of every day should have a point or a purpose. Outside of days when the entire focus is on reviewing material or assessing students, that point or purpose should be to teach a new skill or content. Once instruction is delivered, it is essential to measure its effectiveness or else the time may have simply been wasted.

The following scenario, while simple, has helped to clarify the above point for many teachers I have had conversations with over the past several years.

A video cameraman is sitting in the back of the classroom. The camera-man focuses in on the teacher's every movement and every word. Every-thing the teacher does for a full forty-five minutes is documented by film.

Now imagine that you are watching that film—can you tell whether or not the lesson was effective?

A student-centered teacher's response should be "no." You cannot tell if it is effective unless you can see how students are interacting with the teacher and with the material. Simply put, instruction is a two-way street: what is delivered and what is received. Regardless of how well something may be delivered, if it is not received, it was not effective.

So you can see the need for daily checks to see if students are making appropriate progress toward standard via daily formative assessments. Temperature checks must be taken regularly to determine if the practice of the teacher in the room must change to better support the performance of the children. There are hundreds of techniques to use for formative assess-ment, but below I will highlight a handful of my personal favorites:

♦ **Electronic voting devices**. These are very powerful, progressive tech-supported tools. They allow students to answer questions with complete anonymity and also allow teachers to collect data for the entire class instantaneously.

♦ **Individual whiteboards**. Same concept as above with slightly less anonymity, but with less cost.

♦ **Exit slips**. This is the practice of asking review questions at the end of the class and having students hand in their answers as they exit the classroom. This process can provide global and individual data for teachers.

♦ **High-level questioning**. At its root, questioning is a type of assessment. Teachers that ask rigorous, high-level questions and do not allow non-participation can gain tremendous knowledge regarding student proficiency.

♦ **Mentor/mentee activities**. Creating groups specifically designed for mentor/mentee relationships for given outcomes allows the teacher to form mentoring partnerships through observation of work through assessment, practice, and participation. These relationships and co-ownership of learning can produce remarkable gains in student achievement.

Enrichment Activities

Differentiation, like intervention, should take place whenever the original curriculum and instruction did not meet the needs of the learner. This includes the learner who did not benefit from the instruction because he or she had already mastered the concept. The adult-centered paradigm that it is the responsibility of the teacher to get everybody over this bar—or to proficiency—in a certain area ignores the fact that literally hundreds of thousands of kids sit through school bored each day because the material being taught does not mentally "stretch" them. The student-centered paradigm of seeing the marked growth of each student as the responsibility of the teacher better promotes the planning for and implementation of enrichment activities.

Enrichment activities can take many forms, with each particular scenario calling for a different methodology to be used. A few key components to be considered while planning enrichment include these: enrichment does not equal extra credit; enrichment does not need to be graded differently (this is much easier when standards-based grading is your current method); and don't assume students will instantly scoff at the idea of doing more or harder work. Once you internalize those concepts, you must then figure out how to create a systematic way to enrich student learning on a daily basis.

The following list of strategies is not meant to be exhaustive but illustrative of a handful of the student-centered techniques that can be employed to better educate our students.

- ◆ **Extension of skills**. Extension of skills is the most common manner in which teachers differentiate today. This practice is simply providing students who have shown proficiency in the desired outcome harder or additional work. While the intent of enrichment is never to give students who are doing well more work (therefore punishing them), it can be used as a strategy depending upon when a student shows mastery of the content. This practice is much easier and of considerably more benefit to students when the outcomes align to a standard that clearly identifies how the skills being addressed will increase in rigor in the future.
- ◆ **Peer mentor**. This process of enrichment may be the easiest way to adapt the curriculum for students demonstrating proficiency, although with limited skill advancement offered to the student. In this process, teachers utilize students who have shown proficiency in the area to support the learning of others. While this process may not help students develop new skills, it will often allow students to deepen skills and progress from proficiency to mastery.
- ◆ **Teacher assistant**. Once you have data indicating that some students have proficiency in a certain topic, why not let those students help teach the class? Imagine this:
  Hey Johnny and Alyssa, you two seemed to really understand prepositions on the pre-assessment, so now I need your help. Here is what I plan to teach tomorrow, and this is what I want the rest of the class to be able to do—can you tell me how you would teach it to the students?

  Or

Hey Johnny and Alyssa, you two seemed to really understand preposi-tions on the pre-assessment, so now I need your help. Here are some questions I was thinking of asking on the next test—can you make them harder and provide the answers for me?

Those conversations are just an example, but there are many ways to involve students in the planning and execution of lessons that will naturally deepen and broaden their knowledge in the subject matter.

◆ **Complexity of text.** This enrichment activity can work in any class because literacy is a component of every discipline. Thus, increas-ing the level of text complexity, often denoted by the Lexile level of the reading, is a way to enrich the curriculum for students. For instance, if fourth-grade students are going to be assessed on their ability to write opinion pieces on topics or texts, supporting a point of view with reasons and information, then some students could be asked to read a more complex text. For instance, instead of reading *Secret Garden,* those students may read *Little Women.*

Remediation Outcomes Aligned to the Stated Standard

Most schools and most teachers are still driven by the almighty letter grade. The "A" to "F" grading scale impacts more decisions regarding students than nearly anything else. This fact brings us the third facet teachers must keep in mind when focusing on differentiation. If remediation is needed, it must be remediation *toward* a particular standard—not *for* a particu-lar grade. Often students will be given make-up work or supplementary assignments in order to take their failing grade to a passing one—but the failure to meet the standard, a failure that was represented by the first letter grade, is not addressed. Truly differentiating to student needs means a par-adigm shift toward assessing student proficiency on stated outcomes and away from practices that emphasize grading based on effort and behavior.

Remediation to standard means that students are identified for need-ing additional support based on their performance against set criteria, not based on a grade. To help understand this process, think of the Response to Intervention system (RTI) as a macro version of classroom differentiation. A universal screening tool compares students to their peers by assessing their ability to demonstrate proficiency on a standard. Based on those results, intervention systems may be put into place to support a student's learning.

Remediation in the classroom should look the same way, except on the micro level. All students are assessed on set criteria and the data from that assessment are collected. Remember, this may be as simple as viewing the whiteboards students hold up after doing a practice problem and observ-ing who struggled. Then remediation is offered until students demonstrate proficiency. This process may take ten minutes or ten days. This process may take place with a student who currently is earning a 98% or a student who has a 38%. The process is not grade-based. It is outcome-based and specific to the areas in which students have demonstrated they need additional support.

Preplanned Activities

For differentiation to occur on a daily basis and be systematic in nature, it must be planned for with every lesson. Although some teachers are skilled and adept at transitioning on the fly and providing remediation and enrichment to those in need, differentiation should not just be improvisation. Great teachers embed within their lesson plans, on a daily basis, the four questions that serve to define a professional lesson community (Dufour, 2009):

1. Are we clear about what we want students to know and be able to do?
2. How will we know what students have learned?
3. How will we respond when students do not learn the material?
4. What will we do for the students who already know the material?

To break this down into easier-to-understand chunks, we will examine each question individually and discuss how you can best incorporate each one into a lesson plan.

Are we clear about what we want students to know and be able to do?
- Post and directly state expected learning outcomes at the outset of each class.
- The desired outcomes should be written by students as well (as described on page 24).
- At any point during the lesson, any student should be able to tell you the purpose behind what he or she is learning.

How will we know what students have learned?
- At some point during and at the close of each lesson, some activity must exist so that you (the teacher) can take the temperature of the class.
- This must be a planned experience for students in which data (information) is collected by the teacher and impacts the rest of the class (think of it as a choose-your-own-adventure book).
- How you check student progress must be directly aligned to the purpose of the lesson.

How will we respond when students do not learn the material?

♦ Preplanned activities are at the teacher's fingertips for students who are struggling.

♦ This activity does NOT mean that you state the same material in the same way, just louder and slower (how I differentiated when I first started teaching).

♦ Use activities that explain the material in a different manner— either a different methodology or a different explanation of processes.

♦ Response should be immediate. It is not okay to wait three days before a student receives support for material or skills that were not learned upon original instruction.

What will we do for the students who already know the material?

♦ A plan should exist on how to make the lesson meaningful for students who have already demonstrated proficiency.

♦ This may include a myriad of activities—but it is something that the teacher should be prepared for before it occurs.

♦ The enrichment activity must also pertain to the standard being taught. For example, free reading during a math lesson is not a viable enrichment activity.

STRATEGY

6

Give Students the Right to Choose

Most adults in the country have read enough research, watched enough infomercials, or visited the doctor enough times to know that exercise is important. Despite knowing that exercise is important, many people are still far too sedentary. Can you imagine how many more people would be inactive if the only way we were told we could get exercise was by playing basketball? The point of exercise, if you ask your doctor, is pretty clear: to elevate your heart rate for an extended period of time. It simply does not make sense to limit the choices for an activity that could lead to that end product. It does not make sense for exercise *and* it does not make sense for learning.

There are some non-negotiable items that research indicates must be included in every unit of study. Every unit of study should teach content-rich vocabulary; be outcome-based with clearly-stated objectives, essential outcomes, or standards; and provide students with a level of cultural literacy so that when they leave school they are informed adults. Most educators can buy into all of that but struggle with cultural literacy and what exactly that means. When trying to picture cultural literacy, think of *The Tonight Show with Jay Leno* when they ask people on the street who fought in the Civil War. When somebody responds, "New Jersey and New York," that is a great example of not being culturally literate.

Teachers do a great job doing all three of those things: teaching vocabulary, teaching to standards, and providing a level of cultural literacy to students. However, the issue is that far too often, students are allowed to learn in only one manner. So, just as elevating your heart rate for an extended period of time while using large muscle groups constitutes a good form of exercise, offering such exercise in only one form (playing basketball) will result in far fewer people who will actively engage in the activity. The key element is choice—it is just as necessary in education as it is in fitness. If we want to reach all students, we adults must be the ones to demonstrate flexibility, as opposed to expecting students to continually adapt to adult preferences.

The Common Reality

Teachers have upwards of thirty students in a given classroom, many of whom read at different levels, several of whom have behavioral problems, and a few of whom have disabilities. On top of that, teachers have what feels like fifty new initiatives introduced by administration each year. Teaching is hard. In fact, teaching today may be harder than any other time in history. In addition to being an intensely difficult profession, it is also very personal. Some teachers find something they love and teach it over and over for decades. My belief is that one pet unit exists in every district in the United States. It might be the second-grade book students create about birds, or the fourth-grade rainforest unit, or the sixth-grade cell model, or the ninth-grade timeline of World War I—but it most likely exists within your district at this very moment.

These units are not inherently bad, but what happens is that the content begins to supersede the skill in terms of importance. Hopefully after reading this, you will have a hard time finding a reason that the bird book could not be the animal book in third grade or that the World War I timeline could not become an analysis of common progressions within multiple wars. As we become more outcome-driven and student-centered, content will be forced to take a backseat. This is not to say that it is not important for students to be able to identify the participants in the Civil War (as in the Jay Leno scenario above). But is it necessary to have students memorize the dates of specific battles in a war when most students have a device in their pocket that will give them that information in under ten seconds? In order to create 21st-century learners, we must adopt new common practices that may now be more beneficial to our students than some of the "oldie but goody" lessons of yesteryear.

Example of Excellence

Mr. Nelson is a seventh-grade history teacher in Wachota, Wisconsin. Mr. Nelson is passionate about history. He has always loved reading and learning about history and has developed an absolute love of teaching history. When Mr. Nelson began his career, he wholeheartedly believed that his job as a history teacher was to ensure that each student he taught learned the important dates, facts, and figures associated with United States history. This led to students learning a great deal of information through rote memorization and flash cards, but doing little work toward the standards that focused more on students developing skills that would be transferable to other disciplines. Three years ago, Mr. Nelson decided to make a switch. This switch was very painful for him at first, but now he is a firm believer that he has made the best decision for his students. He committed to teaching the skills students needed to have in order to be able to be successful at the next level and abandoned his content-focused approach.

Mr. Nelson committed to this switch by adopting a tic-tac-toe unit assignment board. See Figure 6.1 (page 50) for an example of what a tic-tac-toe lesson board for a seventh-grade unit on military conflict may look like.

The methodology that Mr. Nelson prefers is to have an anchor lesson in the middle of the board. This is the assignment that all students must do. Then, to complete the unit, the students must do a straight line of activities. This means that students must complete three lessons within the unit. This gives each student four choices as to which cluster of assignments they choose to complete, as demonstrated in Figure 6.2 (page 51).

Mr. Nelson groups the activities in this manner, because he places the most rigorous activities at the bottom of the square, and the less rigorous activities at the top. This ensures that each student either completes three moderate-level rigor assignments or a low rigor, moderate rigor, and high rigor assignment in this unit. Employing this strategy also affords Mr. Nelson the ability to have enrichment assignments on hand for students who are excelling in the course.

Why This Is a Learner-Centered Strategy

In this lesson, Mr. Nelson does a great job breaking away from the confines of the traditional methods of teaching history. He does not rely on the textbook to guide his instruction, nor does he simply default to teaching content in chronological order. Instead, he employs a strategy for differentiation (tic-tac-toe boxes) and does a great job providing student choice and

Figure 6.1 Sample Tic-Tac-Toe Lesson Board

Create a timeline detailing major incidents in the Civil War.	Create a poster with all major military conflicts since 1700 with explanations as to why they occurred in a visually appealing manner.	Write a 3-page biography on one of the following: U.S. Grant, General Colin Powell, or General Patton.
Create a PowerPoint presentation that can be posted to YouTube discussing the most effective U.S. general in the last 115 years.	*Anchor Lesson: Compare and contrast three common causes of war in a 3- to 5-page paper.*	In terms of planning, how was the Vietnam Conflict similar to the first Desert Storm? Explain your answer in a paper.
As societies continue to change, what may be a future cause for war that may not have existed fifty years ago? Explain through a speech accompanied by a PowerPoint presentation.	Create a scenario in which the U.S. could have saved over 10,000 lives and still accomplished the military goal in any conflict that took place after 1900 and a write a paper detailing the plan.	Create a podcast detailing the biggest U.S. military blunder of the past 200 years and how it could have been avoided.

being a learner-centered teacher. His unit doesn't expose all students to the same content, but it exposes all students to rigorous assignments that are thematically linked.

Elements of Quality Units That Give Students the Power to Choose

As alluded to earlier in this chapter, creating units that give students a great deal of choice limits teacher control. Lack of control can cause angst for teachers, and it can also cause lessons to go suddenly off-track. Giving students choice in their learning is a learner-centered strategy, but it will not improve student achievement if you are not committed to these elements:

Figure 6.2 Tic-Tac-Toe Assignment Options

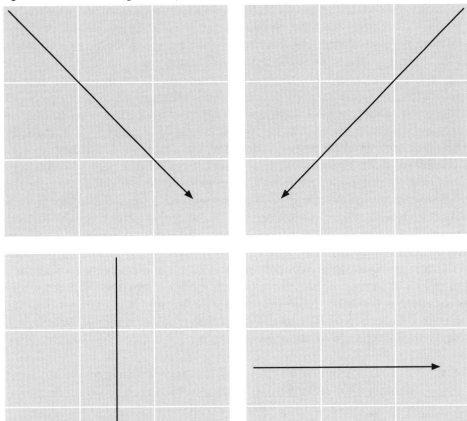

- ◆ Skills-driven assessment
- ◆ Flexible product options for students
- ◆ Flexible content for students to study
- ◆ High rigor for all students

Skills-Driven Assessment

Tremendous amounts of research have been done about giving students flexibility and choice in their learning. From this conversation, two distinct camps have formed, one in favor of student control of their learning and one in favor of a more systematic, regimented approach. One thing both sides can agree upon, however, is that the more engaged students are with their work and the more ownership they have over their own learning, the higher the net results. Transferring this theoretical knowledge to the everyday classroom, however, has proved troublesome for many teachers.

This challenge can be overcome with a strong commitment to skills-based assessment. The key word in the previous sentence is commitment. Many teachers *assess* based on skill/outcome/standard/objective but still *teach* in a content-focused manner. To prove this point, I want each reader to visualize two conversations with the same set of peers or colleagues in your school. One conversation is about the need to change the assessment to make it more rigorous and to align it with standards. The other conversation does not mention the assessment, but begins with a comment about abandoning the "insert favorite unit here." Which conversation would upset teachers the most—the one about changing the assessment or the one about no longer teaching *Romeo and Juliet*? If your subset of teachers would be more upset about the latter than the former, then this tells you that while assessments may be skills-based, teachers are still committed to content.

Committing to skills over content is difficult and becomes increasingly tough as students progress through school. Here are some hints to help you progress forward. Remember that sometimes it is easier to change practice than it is beliefs, and often by changing the practice, beliefs will slowly start to change on their own.

- ◆ **3 to 1 ratio**. For every skill/outcome students are expected to learn, plan for at least three ways in which they could accomplish the goal. This planning forces the teacher to think of multiple ways to address the standard and alleviates commitment to a particular subject of study (content). Notice how much more natural it seems to adopt this practice at the lower grades. Examples include these:
  - If high school students are charged with interpreting graphs and texts about a case study to determine which medical treatment is more effective, they should have the option to study treatments and graphs for a variety of maladies such as high cholesterol, cancer, or asthma.
  - If middle school students are charged with evaluating the way a new disease can impact society, the teacher should seek out contextual information about polio, the plague, and HIV/AIDS, even if the traditional textbook only focuses on one of those diseases.
  - If lower elementary students are charged with making text-to-world connections, the teacher should have a variety of stories for students to read involving characters of different backgrounds and interests.
- ◆ **Self-diagnose**. As teachers, we all have something we are passionate about teaching. My experience as a sociology teacher led me to

think that my unit on stereotypes and every activity within it should be "must-see" for students. In hindsight, although the activities may have been good, they were focused on a particular subgroup of students. I was much more focused on the activity than the skill or outcome I was attempting to teach.

♦ **Survey students**. Ask one or two questions at the end of the assessment asking if the students felt that the teacher did a better job making them knowledgeable about the outcome/standard/ skill or about the content.

Flexible Product Options

Depending on the skill being assessed, you can usually let students choose the product that best allows them to demonstrate their knowledge. Unless the desired outcome deals directly with standards for writing or speaking, as a teacher you have the flexibility to give students options. For example, you can let students demonstrate understanding of the critical components of a narrative-essay through writing, speaking, visuals, or technology-supported presentations. Here are some tips to help you move forward in this area.

♦ Remember the modalities of learning (multiple intelligences).
   • Creating potential product descriptions is made considerably easier if you reflect on these types of learning: verbal, interpersonal, intrapersonal, naturalist, kinesthetic, logical, spatial, language.
♦ Allow students to select a product.
   • You can provide the desired outcome, skill, or standard and allow students to attempt to design a project or assignment that satisfies that requirement.
♦ Create a scoring rubric to ensure grading equity and alignment to a specified outcome.
   • Be completely driven by the outcome. If you are, then it won't be hard to create a scoring rubric that looks the same for an oral report or a collage.
♦ Do not be afraid of technology.
   • Technology allows for many new ways for students to express their learning and mastery of material and skills. Do not let a personal discomfort with technology inhibit students from showing off their 21st-century skills.

Flexible Content for Students to Study

A final reminder: If the skill is what is important, the content can be flexible. The tic-tac-toe diagram presented earlier demonstrates this concept wonderfully. It is no longer essential for students to be able to tell you what date the Battle of Bunker Hill occurred on or what color Juliet's dress was when she died. It is important, however, for students to explain why and how colors of clothes may be symbolic in books and why certain battles were more pivotal because of the time period in which the war took place. Those two things, however, can be taught through a variety of methods, and to increase student engagement and thus (typically) student achievement, students should have a choice.

High Rigor for All Students

Rigor in the educational sense means provoking students to use their critical thinking skills. In order to provide choice for students, the desired outcomes almost invariably must be higher order in nature. Let's examine an example that could be used in a first-grade classroom to demonstrate how higher-order thinking is possible at every level. The following list shows a series of outcomes that progress through Bloom's revised taxonomy. These outcomes are based on the theme of children's book titles:

- ◆ **Knowing**. As a result of this lesson, students will be able to identify the title of the book.
- ◆ **Understanding**. As a result of this lesson, students will be able to tell what the title of the book meant.
- ◆ **Applying**. As a result of this lesson, students will be able to predict the title of a book by listening to its story.
- ◆ **Analyzing**. As a result of this lesson, students will be able to pick a portion of the text that explains why the book was titled in a certain manner.
- ◆ **Evaluating**. As a result of this lesson, students will be able to judge whether the title of the book was the best possible title.
- ◆ **Creating**. As a result of this lesson, students will be able to create a story outline just by hearing the title of a book.

In this brief example of what a first grade teacher could do with the thematic content of book titles, it is clear that the more rigorous the activity, the easier it is to provide students a choice in what they are doing. The higher the level of rigor or critical thought needed, the easier it is for students to have a choice in what they are doing.

STRATEGY

Student-First Homework

Homework, homework, homework—there are plenty of books, professional development activities, and articles discussing this controversial topic. This chapter will not attempt to sway people from any of the homework camps that have strong belief systems. Instead, our intent is to unify the divided subsections of educators and provide tips for all teachers on how they can ensure that their practice is learner-centered moving forward.

Before we continue, it is important for everybody to realize one thing. In conversations with hundreds, if not thousands of educators, when the topic of homework comes up I always pose the question, "Why do you assign homework?" The answer is never, "Because it makes me feel better" or "I like to stress out kids." The answer always revolves around the idea that homework in some form or capacity helps kids master the current material and grow to become better learners. It is important, regardless of which homework camp you reside in, that there is a common understanding that the overwhelming majority of educators assign homework because they believe it will benefit kids. The purpose of this chapter is to make sure that as educators our behaviors align with our philosophy and that our practice serves to accomplish our goal.

The Common Reality

Teachers spend a great deal of time planning and preparing in order to provide students with lessons of high rigor and high relevance in order to best engage the student in authentic learning. With such extreme focus on student performance and increased accountability measures, many teachers find that there is simply not enough time for students to get through all of the material they need to learn in order to be successful. Thus, homework is often assigned. Sometimes the homework is practice over what has already been taught and monitored in class. Other times homework activities are the first opportunities students have to tackle a problem on their own. Still other times, homework is assigned in order to prepare students for the work that will be coming in the near future.

The homework that receives the most attention—by students, parents, teachers, and the greater educational community—is the homework that requires students to produce a product and that is collected by the teacher. This process, in the traditional classroom, involves the assigning of work during class time and the expectation that the work will be turned in the next day. What happens in many cases is that the teacher collects the homework and then begins to teach the next segment of material. The teacher then, during a free period, will go through the homework and do one of three things:

1. Mark answers as correct or incorrect.
2. Mark answers as correct or incorrect and provide specific feedback as to areas of student deficiency.
3. Check for completion and student effort.

This process of homework review sometimes occurs within ten minutes of the homework being turned in and sometimes within ten days. In fact, I have been witness in many instances to homework actually being returned after the assessment of the given subject matter. While this may be an extreme case, what happens commonly is that neither the students nor the teacher is informed quickly enough about students' homework performance to be able to change the course of action and ensure student mastery.

Example of Excellence

Ms. Shawn Shannon teaches third grade in an area of San Diego that has high diversity and has a vast majority of students coming to them from families with low socioeconomic status. Ms. Shannon is currently helping students reach the desired outcome of being able to successfully break down and complete story problems that require the use of simple multiplication facts. Ms. Shannon is technologically savvy and has a strong desire to "flip" the classroom, but is also cognizant that many of her students do not have access to the technology necessary to support this at home, and her school does not have the ability to provide that access for students at this time. Although Ms. Shannon understands this, she does not accept the status quo and goes through the work of publishing each lesson via YouTube for any student or parent who has access. However, she does not require or count on her students to make use of this additional resource.

At the end of the math lesson on Tuesday, Ms. Shannon provides each student with a worksheet that needs to be completed at home. The worksheet is divided by standards or outcomes (or as she refers to them with her students, "I can" statements). On Wednesday, when the math segment of the daily instruction begins, Ms. Shannon posts the correct answers with the work shown on the overhead projector or ELMO. Students are familiar with this routine and once the assignment is posted, they approach the front of the room to get their "special green marking pens." With the green pens, the students go through and self-correct their assignments. While they are going through this process, Ms. Shannon rotates through the classroom with a clipboard, making note of which students are demonstrating mastery and which students are struggling.

After a few moments, the answer sheet posted on the ELMO is replaced with a new, similar worksheet. The teacher then announces the two-person teams that will be working together on the material. The groups are comprised of students who mastered the material and those who struggled with it. This grouping allows for student collaboration and mentoring. The additional fifteen-minute activity is planned for with flexibility. If the vast majority of students perform well on the homework assignment, then the teacher moves forward as a whole group and provides individual remediation at a later time to the student or students who struggled. After the in-class work is complete (approximately ten minutes later), the process repeats itself until Ms. Shannon is confident based on student performance that it is time to move on to the next lesson.

Why This Is a Learner-Centered Strategy

There are many reasons that the above Example of Excellence is learner-centered. First and foremost, the assignment is purposeful. The homework is an activity to not only provide practice but also to provide insight into how students are progressing toward achieving a desired outcome. Additionally, the feedback provided to students is immediate and their performance is factored into the subsequent adult behavior and thus student learning. In an adult-centered environment, the homework would have been collected and returned to the students in due time—in one day, maybe two, maybe more. This potentially leaves some students struggling on an outcome without feedback, supplemental instruction, or remediation for several days.

Elements of Learner-Centered Homework Practice

As discussed earlier, there are definitely different schools of thought on homework and its place in 21st-century education. Regardless of your position, there are four key elements that you can employ in your homework process that embody a learner-centered mentality:

- ◆ Mastery over grades
- ◆ Purposeful homework
- ◆ Homework aligned to outcomes
- ◆ Feedback that informs *the action of* all parties

Mastery Over Grades

When homework is student-centered, its purpose is to facilitate mastery over the desired content or skills. When homework is less driven by what is best for students, the focus often becomes the grade. In many schools throughout the nation, the question of what percentage of homework should count toward a student's overall grade is a highly debated topic. The real question is this: What do particular districts, schools, and teachers think a grade should represent? In a student-centered environment, grades represent what kids know and are able to do based on an established set of criteria. Thus, homework assigned in a learner-centered environment is focused on promoting mastery far more than assigning a grade for the work completed. Teachers must break from the paradigm that for something to be important or meaningful, it must be graded. For something to be important or meaningful, it must help students move forward in their progress toward achieving a goal.

Purposeful Homework

Great teachers, student-centered teachers, always ask themselves before assigning work to a student, "Will this help them better progress toward accomplishing the stated goal?" If the answer is yes, then the homework process can be a student-centered endeavor. If the answer is no, then the homework should not be assigned.

So, what does that mean for teachers? In most cases, one-size-fits-all homework is not student-centered. If a student has already shown you a high level of mastery on a given topic, then assigning more work in that area is not purposeful for his or her educational growth. A good self-checklist you can use when assigning homework includes these three questions:

1. Will the assignment help students master the skills deemed essential for this unit of study?
2. Will the assignment serve to enrich students' learning by extending their current skills or content knowledge?

3. Will the assignment provide me information regarding student progress that will allow me to better serve students moving forward?

If the answer to all three of these questions is no, then the homework is simply not purposeful and should not be assigned.

Homework Aligned to Outcomes

Homework must be directly tied to the desired outcome for students. If every problem or portion of the assignment does not specifically align to what students should know and be able to do in a particular unit, then the assignment should be reconstructed. The common argument against this revision is that although something is not directly stated as essential for a student to know or be able to do, that does not mean that it is not important. If you are thinking that right now, you are correct. However, although you are correct, so too are the educators who want to tell anybody who will listen that there is simply not enough time in the school year to teach kids all they need to know. So yes, whatever a particular teacher—that teacher may even be you—wants to include in a homework assignment is undoubtedly important, but if it is not part of the desired outcome, then it is simply not essential. Until all kids are learning all essential things, we simply cannot consume ourselves with teaching *everything* that is important.

Feedback That Informs the Actions of All Parties

It would be nice to be able to label this section "feedback in 24 hours" or some other arbitrary segment of time. That would give all readers a much more concrete manner in which to move forward, but such uniformity does not serve the best interest of the educational environment in which we live. For instance, the deadline for this book to be finished is in four months. I can submit a draft and await feedback from my editor for a few weeks and still have adequate time to receive the information, process it, and make mid-course corrections so that the end goal of publishing a quality book that will help serve educators is met. This example illustrates the main tenets of prompt, effective feedback:

- Quick enough to impact future learning decisions of the student
- Quick enough to impact future instructional decisions of the teacher
- Thorough enough to support learning of all parties

Future Learning Decisions of the Student
Sometimes you just do not know what you do not know. Think about yourself—you probably have a subject, area of study, or human interest in which you are not strong. For me, I am simply not handy. If I were in a

class whose end outcome was to build a chair, and each lesson went over a specific step or component of building a chair, I would absolutely need feedback on each step before attempting to satisfy the end goal. If I were not given feedback on any component of instruction, I definitively know that I would not want to be the first person to try and take a seat! My chair is another person's tying his shoes, another person's geometric proof, and another person's diagramming a sentence, and another person's balancing of a chemical equation. Feedback must be prompt enough to alert students to know what they do not know so that they can make the necessary mid-course corrections. Teachers must operate from the paradigm that students truly want to be great and that showing students how they can improve will have an impact on the future performance.

Future Instructional Decisions

Feedback must also inform the teacher of what to do next in the class. I joke with teachers I work with about the person who had a lesson plan book for all 174 days and did not deviate from that plan regardless of the circumstance. While that example is hyperbolic, even very good teachers get caught in that trap. When I was in the classroom, I know I got caught myself at times. "I have to give this assessment before midterms come out" or "We cannot possibly spend another day on adding fractions and get through the rest of the material I want to get to" are the types of things all teachers have said or thought to themselves from time to time. But that is exactly the type of adult-centered behavior this book is trying to eliminate. Every piece of work you require a student to do should inform your future practice. This means sometimes speeding ahead and sometimes slowing down. For homework to be meaningful and student-centered, the most important feedback throughout the process is the feedback that the teacher receives regarding student proficiency. This is the most important type of feedback because it impacts the greatest number of students. Another very important teacher self-check when assigning work is asking this question: Will student performance on this assignment directly impact my future teaching? If the answer is no for a given piece of homework, then it most likely is not worth assigning.

Thorough Feedback

This book has already discussed rigor at great length. Simply put, good assignments very rarely have simple right or wrong answers. The reason for that is that good assignments are generally of higher rigor, and the higher the rigor the more variable the potential answers are on a given assignment. Thus, good feedback on good assignments is much more than a simple checkmark, letter grade, or numerical score. Good feedback is thorough enough that students are not left guessing as to what they need to do better on future assignments. A good self-test for teachers here is to review the feedback you provide through the lens of your husband, wife, mother, or father—just choose someone who is not an educator. If that person could be informed by the comment on how to improve an assignment, the comment is good. If that person could not, then the feedback is not learner-centered and would not drive improvement in student achievement.

Flipped Classrooms

It is hard to talk about homework, learner-centered philosophy, and 21st-century learning without mentioning the concept of the flipped classroom. There are many resources that detail the philosophy behind this method and how it can improve classroom instruction and student achievement. Therefore, we will not spend a great deal of time discussing the nuts and bolts of it in this book. What is clear, however, is that the practices that support a learner-first philosophy described above align directly with the concept of flipping a classroom. The focus on student outcomes, prompt feedback, and the ability to be flexible with instruction are simply best practices and should be commonplace—whether in the traditional format or using the flipped classroom concept.

STRATEGY

8

Questioning for Kids

Imagine you are doing some last-minute grocery shopping and plan to get home to watch something that you consider appointment television—this may be anything from *The Bachelor* to a big football game. As you approach the checkout line, you run into an acquaintance with whom you have not had a conversation in quite some time. You reach out your hand, exchange pleasantries, and ask the question, "How have things been?" Your acquaintance, let's call him Steve, proceeds to share with you an honest response to your polite, open-ended question. You learn that he is now out of a job, has recently lost a loved one, purchased a puppy, and found a new significant other online. Now that you are engaged in the conversation, it would be rude to reroute the talk or abruptly end the dialogue. So before you can move on with checking out your items, 25 minutes pass and your once well-construed plans of watching a particular television show have now been significantly altered.

All of this occurred because of one open-ended question. Plans were affected, timelines had to be adjusted, and control over your own environment was temporarily lost. Now flip this situation to a classroom— such a situation may have led to a teacher losing over half of his or her instructional time for a particular lesson. If losing personal time in front of a television is disappointing, losing much-needed instructional time can be downright frightening. Asking open-ended questions of students—regardless of age and content—is a scary proposition for teachers, so we often ask questions in a manner that is comfortable and safe for the adults, not challenging and productive for kids.

The Common Reality

Teachers work diligently to plan lessons aligned to standards. They study the content, find materials and resources that will help kids demonstrate mastery of the material, and create assessments to measure student progress toward that end. Teachers also ask kids questions. In almost every lesson I have ever taught or observed, students at some point are asked questions. The questions asked, however, usually are "check ups" or are based on content. Do a quick self-check—how many times do you ask questions that are very similar in concept to the items below?

- Is everyone okay?
- Can we move on?
- Does everybody feel good about this?
- What color dress was the main character wearing?
- In what year did Columbus sail to America?
- What is the second stage of mitosis?

Those questions are teacher-driven. They are either designed to give the teacher permission to move on with the content or they are designed to check if students can regurgitate factual information. These questions are safe and are designed to help keep lessons moving at the quickest rate possible, not to create the deepest possible level of understanding. The good news is that without additional planning or research, any teacher at any grade level can become a student-centered questioning machine by following a few simple principles of practice.

Example of Excellence

Mr. Hickerson began his fifth-grade science lesson with a six-minute video on the scientific method. After watching the video, students were instructed to write down one question that they would really have to think about what they just watched in order to answer correctly. Students took a few minutes to complete this activity. They had become accustomed to this routine and were motivated to make their questions stand out, because they knew that Mr. Hickerson always picked the best ones to read out loud to the full class. Once the papers were passed forward, Mr. Hickerson went to his drawer and reached for a tightly-bound pile of popsicle sticks with each child's name written on one.

Mr. Hickerson selected the popsicle stick with Chad's name on it first, and he asked Chad to try and think of a one word way to describe the scientific method. The class was quiet, and about five seconds later, Chad said that the scientific method was "like a plan." Two students who thought they had a better answer than "like a plan" raised their hands. Mr. Hickerson reminded the students that they were to raise their hand only when they had a question for him, not an answer. Mr. Hickerson then asked Chad to expound upon his answer and he did so completely. Mr. Hickerson then selected the popsicle stick of Brad and asked him to tell him what the very best part of Chad's answer was. Brad responded, "I don't know." Mr. Hickerson responded by saying that he was asking him to give his opinion, so "I don't know" is not an option. Mr. Hickerson then repeated Chad's original answer and asked Brad the same question again. The class sat silent for about 10 seconds, and then Brad responded with a short critique of Chad's answer.

Mr. Hickerson then directed the students to get into their discussion groups for the next part of the lesson. Students quickly got up and moved their desks to discussion formation. Students were then handed a short reading describing the process one student took to see if paper fell as fast a basketball. Mr. Hickerson then passed a paper out to the groups on which they had to create a chart telling what things the student in the reading did well in terms of following the scientific method and what things he did not do well. As students began to work through this process and discuss the question, Mr. Hickerson began to quickly flip through the student-generated questions in order to be sure that he included one of their questions in the lesson. Mr. Hickerson found the appropriate question and then began to travel through the classroom to monitor student progress. After about fifteen minutes, most students had progressed through the bulk of the first question, and he asked students to flip their paper over and answer this student-generated question: In what class other than science could you use the scientific method?

One group stalled during this time, and Mr. Hickerson had to respond and reteach the scientific method to those students. The other five groups continued on with ease and strong dialogue between group members. After getting the last group on track, Mr. Hickerson called the full class back together to ask some follow-up questions to ensure that students were demonstrating mastery over the objective for the day: analyzing others' use of the scientific method and evaluating the impact of not following proper procedures throughout. As Mr. Hickerson began asking questions, one group of students, Brittany, Tiffany, and Michael, continued their table conversation. Mr. Hickerson pulled a popsicle stick to ask his next question, and even though it read Aly, he asked the question of Tiffany. Tiffany was able to respond to the question appropriately, and this led to the end of the additional talk at their discussion table. As Mr. Hickerson continued to pose follow-up questions, he was confident that the objective of the day was understood by his students and that he did not need to assign supplemental homework practice.

Why This Is a Learner-Centered Strategy

Mr. Hickerson's lesson was entirely focused on students. He introduced the material of the day in a student-friendly and time-efficient manner and then immediately set expectations very high for his students. The expectation was clear that students were to use the information from the video to encourage their thinking for the day. The lesson was based on asking questions and having students provide information, as opposed to the traditional means of the teacher methodically "filling the brains" of the students. In addition, he took chances by asking open-ended questions and allowing students to contribute to the lesson. Judging from the amount of times the kids worked and spoke compared to the amount of times the teacher did, this was an extremely learner-centered lesson.

Elements of Learner-Centered Questioning

In the above lesson, Mr. Hickerson did many things very well. By breaking down the Example of Excellence, it becomes easier to chunk the practice and define the elements of kid-centered questioning. Although the described lesson is a fifth-grade science lesson, the elements of kid-centered questioning can be applied to any age, from kindergarten to post-secondary. The elements are these:

- ◆ Scripted questions
- ◆ Higher-order questions
- ◆ The teacher controls who responds
- ◆ Mandatory participation
- ◆ Every student talks, every lesson
- ◆ Student-created questions

Scripted Questions

Mr. Hickerson's lesson revolves solely around questioning and discussion. While this is positive and most likely would result in significant student learning, it is also understood that there are times when the teacher needs to dispense information to students. Even on those days, the teacher should ask multiple questions. In fact, the teacher should not just ask multiple questions, but multiple open-ended and higher-order questions. The goal when asking questions should not be for students to simply answer the question at hand, but should be to start an intelligent, informed discourse among students.

It is vital not to assume that this is impossible with your students, even if you teach the primary grades, or special education students, or students with high-risk factors. All kids can discuss complex issues. Just last weekend I watched two kids, six and five, spend twenty minutes creating a way that the kids in *Frosty the Snowman* could have worked together to keep Frosty from melting. If these types of conversations can occur without prompting and pre-teaching, they certainly can occur with the prompting of great teachers.

The bottom line: Every lesson, every day should contain five pre-planned (scripted) questions that require critical thought and should lead to true student discussion.

Higher-Order Questions

Rigor and higher-order questions have been a theme throughout the book. Understanding and implementing a rigorous curriculum is essential to produce student-centered instruction. In Figure 7.1 (below), I provide a review of Bloom's Revised Taxonomy and example questions from a unit dealing with Columbus's expedition to the Americas.

In looking at those questions, it becomes apparent that the first three levels of questions could be answered with one word, or at most one sentence. In addition, there are correct answers to those levels of questions. The bottom three levels ask questions that do not have a correct answer, but instead have a defendable answer. By asking those types of higher-order questions, teachers can promote healthy discourse and dialogue in their classes.

Figure 7.1 Bloom's Revised Taxonomy with Sample Questions

Remembering	What were the names of the ships Columbus used to sail to the Americas?
Understanding	What was the original intent of the expedition?
Applying	Why were Native Americans referred to as Indians?
Analyzing	What different steps of preparation would you have taken to better ensure the success of the expedition?
Evaluating	Was Columbus a great explorer? Why or why not?
Creating	Create a plan for exploration as if you were the king of a European country knowing exactly what was known before Columbus began his journey.

The Teacher Controls Who Responds

In typical classrooms when a teacher asks a question, one of four things tends to happen:

1. The teacher does not provide adequate wait time and then answers the question on his or her own.
2. Students respond in a choral manner.
3. A select group of highly-motivated students raise their hands to the point it seems like they may dislocate their shoulder in hopes they get called upon.
4. Nobody volunteers, so the teacher calls on somebody who normally "bails" them out.

None of those methods is good professional practice. Everyone reading this should begin implementing more student-centered questioning techniques as soon as possible. Start with two expectations and one personal change in practice.

- ◆ **Expectation One**. There is no time when shouting out the answer is appropriate. (Please keep in mind that if you are asking higher-order questions, it will naturally deter such behavior.)
- ◆ **Expectation Two**. Students are to raise their hands when they have a question, not in response to having a question asked of them.
- ◆ **Practice Change**. Until calling on non-volunteers becomes second nature, employ the popsicle stick technique. Write each student's name on a popsicle stick and after each question asked, grab a popsicle stick. This allows for built-in wait time and randomness. It is important to not remove a student from the "stack" once he or she answers a question. Great teachers want every kid to be ready to answer every question.

Mandatory Participation

Teachers hope to form productive, respectful relationships with students. Great teachers know that challenging or demeaning students is one way to instantly damage any carefully constructed relationship with a student. Thus, one of the most uncomfortable moments for a teacher (and student) is when the teacher calls on a student to respond to a question and he refuses to participate. Instantly, the teacher is faced with a difficult decision: Do I press and possibly embarrass the student but ensure that he participates and is exposed to the content, or do I permit the student to not participate (and potentially disengage)? From a teacher's perspective, this must appear to be a lose-lose situation.

Although this situation may seem to have no good answer, the answer exists—but it exists well before that moment. Students should be informed on Day One of class or Day One when a teacher decides to improve his or her practice that non-participation will not be accepted. The teacher should not only articulate that it will not be accepted, but should also say *why* it will not be accepted. Even after you've set this expectation, implementing appropriate questioning strategies effectively while preserving relationships is a delicate skill for teachers to learn. Here are some concrete tips for teachers:

◆ Never accept non-participation, but do not force an answer to the question originally asked.
◆ It is the teacher's responsibility to scaffold down the question for students if they are stuck.
  • Original question: Was Columbus a great explorer? Why or why not?
  • Student response: I don't know
  • Teacher response: What would make an explorer great?
  • Student response: I don't know
  • Teacher response: What do you think would make anybody great?
◆ Always be prepared to scaffold down to a simple opinion question. If a student repeats the "I don't know" answer, it is the teacher's job to push the issue because the student does not need to know any background to offer an opinion on the given question.

After utilizing this technique with non-participatory students for a few weeks, experience indicates that the number of incidents requiring a teacher to scaffold down will significantly decrease, as students learn that not participating is no longer an option. It should also be noted, even with specific classroom expectations that *should* prepare a student for an exchange like this, it is always best practice to pull the student aside at a later time and review exactly why you were so adamant about him or her actively participating in the lesson.

Every Student Talks, Every Lesson

Even in small classrooms of 14 to 20 students, it is hard to ask a higher-order question or even a follow-up question to that many students. Great teachers, however, find a way for every student to share his or her thoughts on a topic during every lesson. One strategy all teachers can use to get all students talking is to establish discussion groups as outlined in the Example of Excellence. These are pre-determined groups that students regularly meet in to discuss topics as presented by the teacher. Another strategy teachers can use to get students talking is think-pair-share. It works like this: the teacher presents a question or issue and students have time to think and/or write down their thoughts on the topic, and then they are given time to exchange ideas with a classmate sitting next to them. After the activity is done, the teacher can resume his or her normal questioning strategy, but even if a student is not called upon, he or she has had discussion about the topic at hand with somebody in the classroom.

Student-Created Questions

Truly exemplary, student-centered practice calls for students to be involved in creating discussion topics and questions that spark debate. In this chapter's Example of Excellence, the teacher facilitates this in a very formal manner. Teachers can also promote this simply by creating an open environment within the classroom that promotes discussion. Kindergarten through second grade classrooms are littered with student-created, often higher-order, questions: "Why was the Grinch mean?"; "Could something like no trees growing anymore like in the *Lorax* happen in our town?"; or "Why did it matter that the eggs were green in *Green Eggs and Ham*?" Such questions tend to wane as students progress through school. Great teachers find a way to continue to encourage such openness, thought, and creativity.

Intentional Engagement

Great teachers can make magic happen when helping kids learn. Everybody has had experience with that one man or woman who truly impacts children at an entirely different level. It seems like no matter what combination of students that person is given at the beginning of the year—and we all know that in a given year, the combination of names received on a roster could overwhelm almost anybody—significant learning occurs. By now, you can probably picture who that person is—it may be someone who personally helped you or your own children, or it may be a colleague, or it may even be you.

Now, let's consider the student who has forced teachers from kindergarten through elementary school to pull their hair out. Some pull their hair out in frustration over behavior and antics, and some in desperation to find a way to help the student progress academically. Hopefully, everyone has the image of a student who will remain nameless lodged in their brain—this is a student who is of the "won't do" variety, not the "can't do."

So, when we have a "won't do" student in a classroom where the teacher, even the teacher described in the first paragraph, cannot make magic happen, how do we find success? The key is to get those students one-on-one and work with them individually. It is nearly impossible to willfully disengage in a situation that calls for continual and monitored active participation.

Nothing we have just said is new, or is something that almost any educator could not tell you. But the issue is that we have largely failed to transfer the knowledge learned from successful one-on-one experiences with even the most difficult-to-work-with students to our everyday practice. Every teacher I know wants engaged students and wants to do anything it takes to help students learn. This chapter helps break down what we know about student engagement and what we have learned through successful experiences engaging hard-to-reach students. We hope this will serve as a guide for teachers who are interested in making student engagement a more intentional part of their daily practice.

The Common Reality

The vast majority of teachers create lesson plans for each day. Some of those plans may be two to three typed pages, other may fill a two by two square in a lesson plan book, and others are as simple as a mental plan or chicken scratches on a piece of scrap paper. While their formats may differ, almost all teachers walk into each class, each day with a plan for how they are going to help kids learn.

Let's take a moment to review what the most intricate lesson plan templates generally include:

- ◆ Objectives or outcomes
- ◆ How those outcomes align to standards
- ◆ Introduction or anticipatory set
- ◆ How and what is going to be taught
- ◆ How students may practice it
- ◆ How the teacher will know if students understand the material (formative assessment)
- ◆ How the lesson will be wrapped up

How many of those lesson plan components have to do with student engagement? The introduction or anticipatory set is designed to pique interest, commonly associated with engaging students, but it is not the same concept. For students to be engaged, they must be interacting with the content and/or developing a specific skill. This is possible during an anticipatory set, but more often than not that is a time when the teacher is actively working to excite students about a new concept while students passively listen. The only components of the above lesson plan that truly speak to engaging students are the portion where students practice the material and when the teacher formatively assesses whether or not the students understood the material.

Too often as educators we simply hope to engage students, but we often do not do anything intentional to ensure students are actively interacting with each other, with adults, with the content, or with some other medium. I believe wholeheartedly that teachers work to make the subject matter they are teaching each day interesting. But interesting material and delivery does not equate to a strategic plan to engage students. The best way to make material engaging is to change your paradigm from the deliverer of information to the facilitator of learning. This shift makes all the difference

Example of Excellence

The title of this chapter is intentional engagement. The title alludes to the fact that much of what makes an exemplar in this area are things that take place prior to students ever entering the door. Engagement, then, which teachers often think about in terms of being interesting and entertaining for kids, has little to do with the actual "performance" that takes place in the "sage on a stage" model of teaching, and more to do with preparation and planning. The following Example of Excellence is conducted in the format of an interview to give the reader a peek into what an exemplar teacher would do to best prepare to make her class engaging.

Mrs. Young is a seventh-grade social science teacher in an urban area just outside of Dallas. Although the school's demographics are often referred to as "challenging" or "high-risk, Mrs. Young proudly states that what she has found is that kids are kids and that she has been privileged to teach the students whom she has been assigned. For the better part of twenty years, Mrs. Young has been revered in the community and known as the teacher who can truly get through to even the most hard-to-reach students. Mrs. Young's response to how she does it underscores her skillful teaching, but also provides a pretty sound summary: "I try and stay creative, I make them be creative, and they are always busier during the class period than I am."

When Mrs. Young is asked to go into detail, she states that she has always just planned a little bit differently than everybody else. She said that she starts with a desired outcome and then designs the rest of the lesson by segmenting the class into five-minute phases. She states that the five-minute phases does not mean that she covers each segment of the lesson in that amount of time, but that students never go longer than five minutes without interacting with the material in some way. Interaction, especially well-planned interaction between student and content, more often than not leads to engagement.

Mrs. Young is asked what else she does that sets her apart from her colleagues. Although she is very hesitant to answer, because she thinks her colleagues do an outstanding job, she says that when kids come back they tell her that she did two things much different than everybody else. The first thing that the kids tell her when they come back, she says with an embarrassed smile, is "Although you are older, you are not afraid of the Internet and technology." Mrs. Young expounds, "If a doctor told you that there were new ways that he could possibly treat a sick patient, but he was unwilling to explore them because he thought it would be hard or it was out of his comfort zone, he would not be a doctor very long." She feels the same way about learning. "If I go to a conference, read a book, or even go on Twitter (she giggles at her new tech awareness) and hear that there is a new way that I can help my students learn or develop a love of learning, then it is my responsibility to try and bring it back to my classroom—even if it takes me an hour and a half to figure out Skype when it takes my grandson five minutes."

Mrs. Young is then asked about a "creativity pledge" that a lot of kids talk about. Again giggling, Mrs. Young explains that it is not a pledge, but every single day in every class the benefits of being creative are discussed. She says that after the first four weeks of school, all she has to say is, "We practice being creative, because . . ." and then in choral response the students give the three reasons she had been giving them since the beginning of the year (outlined later in the chapter). Mrs. Young notes that that process is a way of norming her classroom and encouraging a desired behavior daily, until it just becomes "what they do in Mrs. Young's classroom."

Why This Is a Learner-Centered Strategy

Being intentional about engaging students, as Mrs. Young describes above, is about taking the focus off of the content and off of the teacher and placing it directly upon the interaction of the students with what is to be learned. This process is the very definition of student-centered and it begins with a paradigm shift in planning. An engaging teacher is no longer someone who has a tremendous presence, dresses up in the clothing of the times, or has a talent for telling stories. An engaging teacher is one who removes focus from himself or herself, and places the focus on establishing a climate and a culture where students expect to interact with the material at hand and do so creatively.

Elements of Intentional Engagement

As we described in the Example of Excellence with Mrs. Young, intentional engagement focuses around planning and other activities that primarily take place outside the presence of children. This is by no means meant to undercut the importance of being a wonderful instructor in front of kids, but hopefully it speaks to the core of the issue and inspires all teachers to know that they can work systematically to improve the engagement level of their students through:

◆ Planning
◆ Interaction
◆ Culture of creativity
◆ Shift from instructor to facilitator
◆ Exploration of different mediums

Planning

Simply put, planning means keeping kids actively engaged with the material and not just distributing information. In the Example of Excellence, Mrs. Young discusses her concept of five-minute phases. An example of how anybody could plan in that format is provided in Figure 9.1 (below). Note: Your phases don't have to be exactly five minutes.

Figure 9.1 Planning in Five-Minute Phases

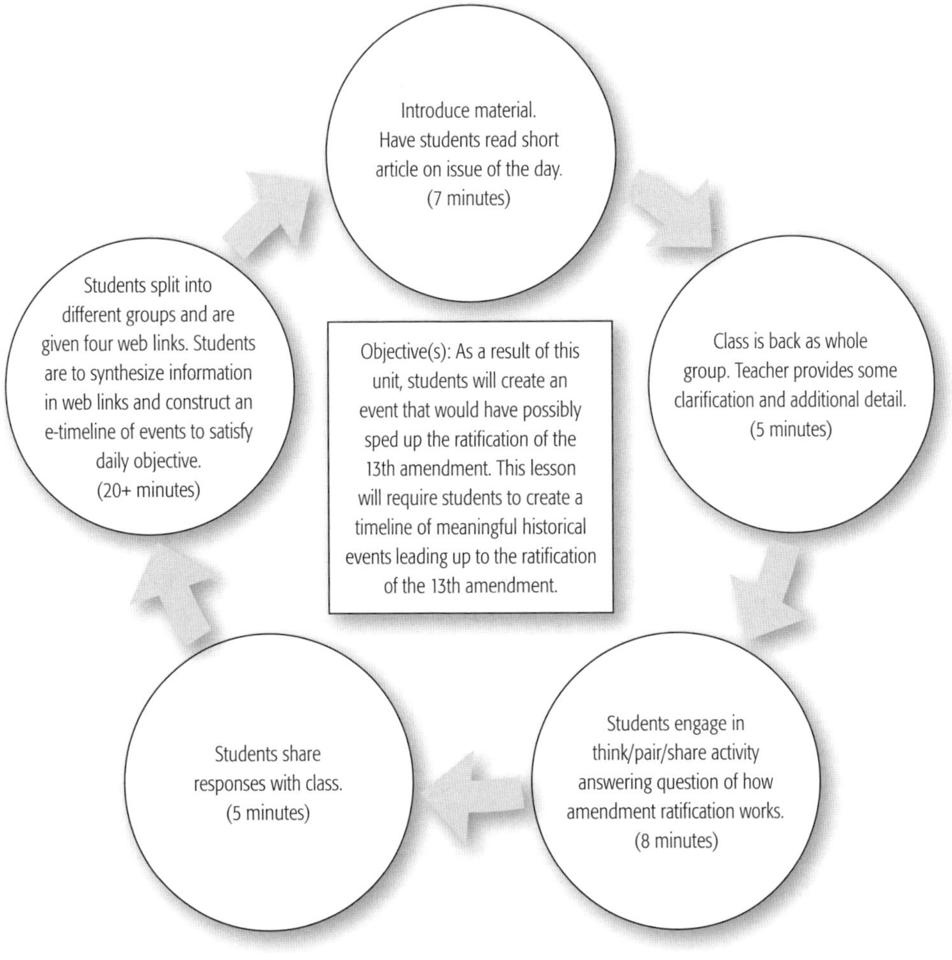

Introduce material. Have students read short article on issue of the day. (7 minutes)

Students split into different groups and are given four web links. Students are to synthesize information in web links and construct an e-timeline of events to satisfy daily objective. (20+ minutes)

Objective(s): As a result of this unit, students will create an event that would have possibly sped up the ratification of the 13th amendment. This lesson will require students to create a timeline of meaningful historical events leading up to the ratification of the 13th amendment.

Class is back as whole group. Teacher provides some clarification and additional detail. (5 minutes)

Students share responses with class. (5 minutes)

Students engage in think/pair/share activity answering question of how amendment ratification works. (8 minutes)

Interaction

This chapter has often described students interacting with others or with material as synonymous with engagement. Let's consider some examples of what student interaction may look like.

Student Interaction with Others
Discussion and Answering: Both of these activities are generally whole-class activities that occur with the teacher leading the process. These two concepts are related, but it is important to note that discussion is a higher-order form of answering, which is also an example of student interaction with others and/or the material at hand. Teachers can dictate what occurs in a classroom—having students answer a question or beginning a discussion by carefully choosing the questions that are being asked. Discussion does not generally occur around a lower-order question, whereas answering can. Let's use the presidency of the United States as the platform:

> Answering: Who was the 33rd president of the United States?
> Discussion: Who was the best president of the last fifty years and why?

Although discussion is clearly the preferred methodology, having students simply answer questions and holding them to the standards set forth in the previous chapter is a way to engage them with the material—just not the optimum strategy. To simplify this, just ask this question: What is more engaging, sitting through a 50-minute lecture or responding to lower-order questions throughout a 50-minute lecture? Most everyone can agree the latter is the better option for engaging students.

Collaborating: This method forces students to interact with each other and the material. Effective collaboration is a learned skill that many students need to be taught. It is important to teach students, even at an early age, that arriving at consensus and truly collaborating to form the best product is not always the same thing. To use the question above, if four people out of a seven person group think that Ronald Reagan was the best president in the last 50 years, but do not provide any substantive evidence, then although gaining consensus around Reagan may be easy, truly collaborating to form the best answer for the group may be very difficult. As mentioned in Figure 9.1 (page 75), think/pair/share is a great way to familiarize students with the sharing out process and the delivery of a singular answer. Consistent activities that are minor and usually ungraded help to form positive habits among students when it comes to collaboration.

Web tools: Teachers must remember that interacting with others does not have to mean others within the same room. The tools provided to teachers via the Internet are nearly endless. Whether it be a chat room, Skype conversation, or Twitter chat, there are many ways in which students can interact with others around a given topic.

Student Interaction with the Material
Reading: Students reading silently in class is evidence of good teaching as long as students are called upon to show comprehension and vocabulary development as a result of the reading. Far too many teachers fear that if an administrator walks in to observe their students interacting with material through silent reading, it will reflect poorly upon them. But nothing is needed more in public school classrooms than teachers who emphasize, promote, and require students to read and write on a daily basis.

Watching: Movies can be engaging and can create substantive memories for people. An entire generation of young women can now tell you a good deal of facts about the events leading up to the sinking of the Titanic. While that movie may not be the most historically accurate or complete depiction, it did serve to promote awareness of a historical event and create lasting recall for a number of people who may otherwise not been exposed to the material. While *Titanic* may be a poor example of what should be shown at school, the point is that showing students clips of movies (usually not movies in their entirety) can improve engagement and student learning.

Writing: There is no other academic process that requires a better synthesis of thought and fewer material resources than writing. In terms of college and career ready skills, literacy is paramount. Literacy in reading and writing must be a focus of all classrooms moving forward. As is true for reading, the process of writing must continue to re-emerge as a focus of classroom activity and not be left as a task to be completed at home.

Creating: When a student is charged with producing something new or different that expresses understanding of the material, learning is at its peak. The ability to take many different thoughts and constructs, some abstract and some concrete, and create them into something new is a skill that, when taught well, stays with a child forever. It is important to remember why creating is at the top of Bloom's Revised Taxonomy and also to reflect on the fact that teachers cannot be an intricate part of the creating process if it is going to be successful. So we can infer that the activities that cause the most significant learning require the teacher to not be an active participant in the process—the activity must be focused around the students and their personal activities.

Culture of Creativity

Being creative is scary, especially for older students. What if my creative ideas are bad or even get laughed at? This is a common thought for adults in work environments; now add the pressure of being a teen or pre-teen among your peers and this becomes a daunting task. One of the most important ways for teachers to increase engagement is to work on creating a culture of creativity in their classrooms—because without specific attention paid to building this culture, it will not organically occur in most classrooms. For a value to become part of the culture of a classroom, it has to become something that "just occurs" within a classroom.

In Mrs. Young's class, the creativity "pledge" (below) was simple but communicated the importance of the skill students would be practicing.

"We practice being creative because
- ♦ Creativity is a skill, not a talent;
- ♦ Creativity is necessary to be highly successful in all jobs;
- ♦ Creativity requires us to think and to truly understand what we are trying to accomplish;

and

- ♦ If no new thoughts or ideas are created in this world, it would be a pretty boring place."

This pledge not only focuses on why the teacher is going to push kids out of their comfort zone, but also acknowledges that nobody is naturally better than anybody else at being creative (this may or may not be scientifically accurate)—so it is something that they are all going to get better at together.

Shift from Instructor to Facilitator

This has been a theme of this book. Once a teacher accepts his or her primary role as the facilitator of student learning as opposed to the instructor of material, then learner-centered instruction will truly begin to occur. The person with the most knowledge about a specific subject area is not necessarily the best teacher. Think back to some of your college professors—they may have known everything there is to know about composition, geology, or Middle Eastern art, but may not have been able to teach a lick. The teacher who understands how best to help other human beings learn, and who also has the necessary knowledge regarding the subject area, is much more effective.

Exploration of Different Mediums

An oft-bandied-about quotation from David Thornburg is, "Any teacher that can be replaced by a computer, deserves to be." Whether you view this statement as pro-teacher or anti-teacher, it is nonetheless thought-provoking. Teachers are often undervalued, and the assumption that software or technology can replace them and produce as viable or more viable graduates is nonsensical to me. However, this quotation sets up a teacher versus virtual teacher conflict. For education to truly move forward, it must be a teacher and virtual teacher partnership that is formed to enhance and energize student learning. I will synthesize my views by picking on Khan Academy, since most educators have heard of this exponentially growing, free website. One hundred out of one hundred times, I would rather a public school teacher provide math instruction to my child than Khan Academy, **but** one hundred times out of one hundred, I would rather my child's math instructor integrate technology and software-based instruction such as Khan Academy into their instructional repertoire. Some Internet resources all teachers should strive to incorporate into their lessons include these:

- ◆ Twitter
- ◆ Evernote
- ◆ YouTube
- ◆ Google Docs
- ◆ Khan Academy (Predominantly math) (www.khanacademy.org)
- ◆ Flipped Classroom sites
  - • Kleinspiration: The Foundation for Flipping Flipped Learning (www.kleinspiration.com)
  - • Flipteaching (www.flipteaching.com)
  - • Chemistry teacher Brian Bennett's website (BrianBennett.org)

STRATEGY

Connection, Not Compliance: Kid-Centered Classroom Management

New teachers receive professional development on student discipline. Almost every school house has a go-to book, set of instructional videos, or annual conference that newbie or rookie teachers are ushered to as part of their mentoring process. Once the original thrust of information about discipline and classroom management is complete, talking about discipline in a school often becomes taboo. Administrators do not like discussing it with teachers because any professional development that encourages increased ownership of discipline problems inside of the classroom, as opposed to in the principal's office, has the potential of making administrators sound unsupportive. Teachers do not like discussing discipline with administrators because if they give the impression that they cannot control their own class, they may wind up with an increase in administrator attention or a negative mark on an evaluation. As a result, a critical segment of schooling and professional development is often swept under the rug for any teacher who is not new or who does not display overt deficits.

Think about how teachers in your building would respond to this statement: When an administrator becomes involved in disciplining your students in the classroom, your management plan has failed. This is a powerful sentiment, one that makes most educators tilt their heads and think for a moment. There are a few statements in education that when truly thought about, analyzed, and internalized can be paradigm altering. This is one. True, sincere belief in the statement means that the teacher has taken complete ownership for all things occurring within his or her class-room. This statement elicits many instant reactions from many educators, such as "How can I control who comes late to class?" and "How can I make sure not one student acts up all year?"

For those questions, there are two simple answers. To address the first issue of students coming late to class, I think a simple data analysis will prove that a percentage of teachers in each building have nearly zero students who arrive tardy on a daily basis. It is important that exemplars are not ignored—they help prove to everyone that true student-centered actions can have a noticeable, data-supported impact upon student behavior. As for the second question, it indicates a failure in classroom management—because a referral to the office means that the actions that took place within the classroom did not adequately discourage the negative behavior. Again, exemplars exist in even the most difficult schools. Great relationships, coupled with firm and fair expectations, can make a difference and help turn the process of managing a class into a process of building relationships that support student learning.

The Common Reality

In most classrooms throughout the country, the vast majority of students go to school to learn, and they follow the rules set forth for the classroom. The fact that most students do what they're supposed to, coupled with the enormous job teachers have to teach massive, rigorous curricula, leads to mere compliance being the goal in most classroom management scenarios. This makes sense. If around 80 percent of students, or hopefully more, are in class to learn, it becomes easy to just want the other students to comply so that you can best teach the students who want to learn. This is one way to manage the classroom.

However, the focus in this situation is on accomplishing what the adult needs to do—not on forming relationships that will help support student learning in addition to establishing a warm, friendly classroom where students behave appropriately. When the goal of a teacher becomes to have a quiet, compliant classroom, the overarching goal of enacting the mission or vision of the school—which usually speaks to preparing students for responsible citizenry—is lost. The term "classroom management" itself lends to the idea that kids are to be managed, rather than to the idea of fostering relationships. For a teacher to truly adopt a learner-centered philosophy, he or she must not only think about this in terms of instructional methods, but in terms of all strategies employed in the classroom.

Example of Excellence

Mr. Tim Varney is a high school English teacher in the inner-city of Miami. The school where Mr. Varney works is among the lowest-achieving in the state and is plagued by violence (inside and outside of school), drop-outs, and a myriad of gang-related issues. In an eight-period high school day, teachers estimate that there is an average of three fights. The teachers clarify the data they provide by stating that there may be two or three days in a row without incident, but on certain days there seems to be at least one fight every passing period. The school also has a large issue with in-school truants. A large number of students attend school but do not go to class. Some wander the halls, others congregate in areas such as stair wells and locker rooms, and others are more blatant about being in the building without any intention of heading to where they are supposed to be.

On paper, this would appear to be a very difficult place to teach—especially in terms of managing a class. Mr. Varney makes it look easy, however. His colleagues marvel at the fact that not only do students not fight in his classroom, but they do not even fight in his area of the building. Although many students spend much of the day wandering the hallways, students actually will run to be inside Mr. Varney's class before the tardy bell. This is not because of his strict enforcement of the discipline code; in fact, Mr. Varney has never written a referral.

Mr. Varney's strategy is actually quite simple: He makes an effort every single day to show kids that he cares about them. He says hello in the hallway, pulls them aside when their mood is off, and views his position with kids as a partner, not as a controller. He also thinks of his job as an educator of kids more than a teacher of English. He takes the time to weave life lessons into the curriculum and to make every lesson relevant to the students now and in the future. He shares responsibility with his students as a partner, not only in terms of their academic progress, but also in terms of their behavior. Classroom expectations are high, but Mr. Varney has established rules that give him the discretion to make decisions based on the best interest of the student as opposed to on the black and white guidelines provided in a handbook or discipline code. While establishing rules in his class to provide wiggle room, Mr. Varney is careful to iterate that although his system does not rely on the school discipline code, it does support the rules established.

Even Mr. Varney, however, has experienced troubling behavior from students. When he does, he says that he does not reinvent how he chooses to do things, but instead goes back to what he does best. He says that he tries to re-establish the relationship and get to the core of the behavior. If a student is acting out, there is a reason. Mr. Varney explains that the reason may be that the child is hungry, scared, or any other non-school related issue, or it may be that he personally has done something to insult or offend the student. In any situation, however, he feels it is his responsibility to get to the core of the issue so that he can change the approach to better reach the individual student. Despite this philosophy, there are times when Mr. Varney needs help. He says that is when he involves counseling and administration. His view is that sometimes he must understand the context of the situation to better serve his students.

Why This Is a Learner-Centered Strategy

Mr. Varney clearly views student behavior as his responsibility. It is not just his responsibility to respond to negative student behavior but also to create the culture within the classroom so that misbehavior does not occur. Each element of what makes Mr. Varney an exemplar revolves around him working to better serve his students. There is no mention of him needing students to behave so he can "get through the curriculum" or so they can achieve higher scores on assessments he or the school cares about. His intention is pure—to best serve the students.

Elements of Learner-Centered Classroom Management

Let's break down Mr. Varney's philosophy into a concrete set of strategies that you can implement. It is important to remember that a change in belief or paradigm can change behavior, but a change in behavior can also serve to change the belief system of the practitioner.

Think of this scenario: the doctor tells you that if you drink more water, many of your daily ailments will go away. You do not believe the advice you have been given and ignore it for several weeks. With your common ailments continuing, you decide to give the doctor's advice a chance. Within a week, you can feel noticeable results. Once you see the results, your belief system begins to change. The same can happen in teaching (or any other profession). Begin by being open-minded and changing the behavior, and often the positive results will serve to change the belief system or mindset.

Some concrete strategies all teachers can use to adopt a learner-centered classroom management philosophy include these:

- ◆ Collaboratively-established guidelines
- ◆ Citizenship and character
- ◆ Independent system of rewards and consequences
- ◆ Administrative partnership

Collaboratively-Established Guidelines

The partnership mindset must prevail, even from the first day of school. This is the first step to changing the common view of the teacher as the

Figure 10.1 Classroom Rules vs. Guidelines

Rules	Guidelines
No food or drink allowed.	Respect your environment.
Do not speak when others are speaking.	Respect your peers.
Overt attention-seeking behavior will not be tolerated.	Respect yourself.
Do not talk back or act defiantly toward the teacher.	Respect all adults in the room.

authority figure and students as subjects. Teachers, remember that generally over 80 percent of your class wants to do well and be part of a learning environment that will allow them to be productive and successful.

It is also important to look at the terminology used in the section—established "guidelines," not rules. The language choice may seem like semantics, but it is not to kids—and actually, it is not to adults. Fill in the blanks: When a rule is broken, the next step is _____. The common reaction to filling the blank most likely has to do with a consequence. Rules imply consequences. Guidelines describe the intended behavior. Additionally, rules generally are written as *what not to do*, whereas guidelines are written from the perspective of *what to do*. Examples of common classroom rules versus guidelines are provided in Figure 10.1 (above).

The examples in the table address very similar behavior, with the exception being that the guidelines allow for a wider interpretation and can serve to deter additional unwanted behaviors. As stated earlier, these guidelines should be collaboratively developed, but we think it is always prudent that teachers realize they are large collaborators in that process and can lead students down a path that creates guidelines consistent with a great learning environment. Examine the guidelines in the table and compare it to the set of classroom rules already established in your own classroom—is there anything that is non-negotiable in terms of expectations that does not fit into the four larger areas of respect delineated above? Moving forward, teachers should employ two concrete strategies:

◆ Use a collaborative process to determine classroom guidelines.
◆ Replace rules with positively phrased guidelines, remembering that less is more when it comes to establishing classroom standards. Guidelines must be written in a flexible manner that allows for teacher discretion at all times.

Those two subtle changes will help frame the classroom in a more student-centered light, immediately impacting both students and teacher.

Citizenship and Character

Classroom policies and management philosophies should focus on students' behaviors as future citizens and on their overall character—and this should be discussed with students. At the very forefront of all school responsibilities is to systematically work to create a productive citizenry. This should not be ignored when it comes to classroom management or in-class discipline. This provides the *why* for students, and the *why* is not "because I said so."

Which of the two scenarios below is more likely to deter the unwanted behavior from occurring again while also serving to strengthen the partnership between student and teacher?

◆ **Scenario One**: Jimmy is talking with his friend Sara in the back of an eighth-grade science classroom when students have been directed to work independently on their homework. The teacher, seated at her desk, asks Jimmy to stop talking, and he does. Two minutes later, the behavior repeats itself. The teacher looks up and simply says, "Jimmy" in a firm voice. Jimmy responds with, "But, Mrs. ———" before he is cut off. "Jimmy, you will not talk back to me and if you talk one more time, you will have earned yourself a discipline referral." Two minutes later, when the same behavior occurs, the teacher directs Jimmy to go to the office and the subsequent paperwork is delivered shortly thereafter.

◆ **Scenario Two**: Jimmy is talking with his friend Sara in the back of an eighth-grade science classroom when students have been directed to work independently on their homework. The teacher walks over to Jimmy and asks what is going on. Jimmy informs the teacher that Sara does not get what was taught today, and he is trying to help her. The teacher says that Sara can come up to his desk so he can help her. He asks Jimmy how he could have handled the situation differently. Jimmy says he does not really see anything wrong with what he was doing, but maybe he could have asked if he and Sara could have gone in the hallway so their talking did not disturb anybody else. The teacher confirms that would have been a good idea, but also says "While what you were trying to do (help Sara) should be commended, if in the future you are doing something that is 'good' but contradicts what your boss says, it may not be good for you." Jimmy nods, the two exchange a fist bump, and the teacher has Sara come up to his desk for some additional help.

That scenario clearly plays out the differences between being rule- and compliance-centered versus student-centered and character-driven and shows how interactions within the classroom may look very different. In Scenario One, the teacher is entirely within her rights to send the student to the principal and write a referral. The student broke the rule, was warned, and chose to break the rule again. The opportunity to build character, remediate the negative behavior, and build future problem-solving skills was completely lost—not to mention the negative impact this could have on student-teacher rapport.

To summarize, student-centered teachers look at discipline issues and first seek to understand what is taking place and seek to understand the child. Teachers who are rule-centered and compliance-focused maintain a laser-like focus on being understood, and students understand there are consequences when rules are broken.

Independent System of Rewards and Consequences

It is hard to imagine a school that does not have a documented consequence system in place to handle student behavior. This compulsion for documentation and student management may be more grounded in litigious reasons than in philosophy, but it still exists. Additionally, many schools have also adopted a proactive means of rewarding students for positive behavior. Schools go about this in different ways, including adding recess time, bringing in a guest speaker, or adding an afterschool dance for those students who have modeled appropriate behavior. While these systems are to be applauded, the fact they exist does not mean that those are the only systems that should. Each classroom should have an independent system of rewards and consequences that operate within the parameters set forth by the overarching building policy.

Some successful systems create rewards for the individual and whole group. While group rewards may be appropriate in some instances, creating group consequences violates much of what educators know to be effective in deterring negative behavior and should not factor into management planning. In creating rewards for a whole group, it is important never to compromise the most effective instructional strategy or to compromise instructional time in doing so. For instance, allowing students to work collaboratively or showing a film is not an ideal reward. True student-centered decisions should never compromise what is believed to best benefit student learning. Possible rewards for whole-group behavior include, but are not limited to these:

- ◆ Allowing students to wear iPods during independent work
- ◆ Permitting students to eat or drink during class
- ◆ Allowing students to select their seats or groups
- ◆ Offering student choice of how material is presented (if the teacher has no viable evidence demonstrating one is superior)

Possible rewards for individual student behavior include, but are not limited to these:

- ◆ Personal phone calls or letters home
- ◆ Individual privileges (iPods, food, etc.)
- ◆ Tangible rewards of negligible cost (I have seen $1 rubber chickens become incredible motivators.)
- ◆ Peer leadership roles

Providing consequences for students should always be done on an individual basis and should always focus on two concepts at once—deterring the negative behavior *and* building a positive relationship with the student. When trying to accomplish those two things, it is difficult to imagine how writing a referral to an administrator without trying other things first accomplishes that. It is also important to note that extreme incidents of student misbehavior—violence, threats, student-to-student bullying—need to be dealt with immediately and administration needs to be involved. For all other incidents of what can be viewed as traditional/typical classroom disturbances and issues of student misbehavior, you should follow this progression of action steps:

- ◆ Address the issue respectfully with the student.
- ◆ Have a private conversation with the student.
- ◆ Have a student/parent/teacher conversation and/or get counselor involvement.
- ◆ Get administrator involvement.

Administrative Partnership

A principal walks into a teacher's classroom and finds the teacher directly violating a stated directive. The administrator waits until there is a natural break, pulls the teacher to the side of the room, and informs the teacher that discipline will follow. The principal returns to her office and writes up a detailed report about what happened and e-mails it to the superintendent. The superintendent calls the teacher in for a meeting. During this meeting, the superintendent gains an understanding as to why the teacher was violating the directive and then assigns what he feels is appropriate discipline. The teacher then returns to his classroom as usual and does not speak to the principal until the next time she happens to observe his class.

That scenario seems like a ridiculous process for teacher discipline, and it would almost certainly erode any trust built between the building administration and faculty and staff. This metaphorical story always receives comments from groups of teachers I am working with that include, "That would never work," "The principal has no ownership or knowledge of the situation," and "The behavior may stop, but the teacher would never respect the principal if that is how it was handled." While it seems ridiculous to handle adult situations in this manner, this is exactly how most schools handle student situations.

Great teachers never simply pass their students up the referral pipeline to deal with administration. After all, what consequence or discussion can an administrator give that a teacher cannot? In most situations, administration can suspend students (inside or outside of school) and expel students. Other than that, all things that administration can do, so too can teachers. This includes personal conversations, contacting parents, involving counselors, before- or after-school detentions, and a myriad of other character-building exercises. When great teachers involve administration with incidents of classroom misbehavior (with the exception of the most egregious incidents), they do so by reaching out to form a partnership to best support the student and to involve one more person in the problem-solving process. Great teachers view involving administration as if they are bringing in a "Big Brother Mentor," whereas discipline-seeking teachers view bringing in administration in the same manner a frazzled parent tells their child, "You just wait until your mother/father gets home and hears how you have been acting." There is a discernible difference in intent and the symbolism of how administration can support a teacher working with a difficult student. Simply put, great teachers want to solve the issue to benefit the child, whereas others hope that the administration and the consequence can force the child into temporary compliance.

STRATEGY

11

Seek Feedback

Receiving feedback is a very scary proposition for many educators. For some reason, the natural evolution of the profession has precluded this from being a normal facet of daily life. Teaching has been a very private and intensely personal act for many teachers for a long time. Think about this scenario and whether it would be scary for you:

- ◆ You work with students throughout a semester.
- ◆ After every fifth day, the students are assessed.
- ◆ You are able to research previous editions of the assessment, but each week it could change.
- ◆ The assessment will try to judge and exploit student weaknesses.
- ◆ While students take each assessment, many of the parents and some community members watch.
- ◆ Sometimes there is even a radio transmission narrating what is occurring.
- ◆ The following morning after the test, all of the relevant data is aggregated and disaggregated and posted in the local newspaper.

This is scary—and this is what a high school football coach experiences each week of the season. This is pretty much the definition of high stakes.

Since a coach experiences such high stakes, think about how he prepares for each game. See if you can make a link to the classroom and understand the lessons to be learned. A coach must do these things:

- ◆ Assess each week how each player on the team is performing
  - He does not make the assessment as an individual, but with a collection of people.
  - He must assess based on evidence (film, statistics) and not on feelings.
- ◆ Compare the strengths of the team to the strengths of an upcoming opponent
  - He must design ways to accentuate their strengths and quickly remediate deficiencies.
- ◆ Establish communication systems to seek out player feedback and input

Athletics can be polarizing among educators. Some people feel that too much time and emphasis are placed upon them, and others feel they are a valuable supplement to a child's education—and some even view athletics as a viable intervention, showing data to support that involvement in athletics is of value for students, especially students with high-risk factors. Regardless of what side of the argument someone endorses, the process by which coaches seek feedback and analyze the information available to them is a practice that would improve many educators' ability to impact student achievement.

The Common Reality

The most stressful times of year for teachers are often these two weeks: evaluation week and the week test scores are released. A lot of people outside the world of education view this as the educators' fear of being held accountable for the results they help to produce. Being around thousands of educators over the past year alone, that is simply not the case. The football analogy above works in many ways, but in many ways it does not. Teaching and learning cannot be quantified in wins and losses. Ask any third-grade teachers who have helped a non-reader read, even though he will not "pass" the state test, whether they feel their worth is judged by a standardized test score, and they will scoff. Teaching is the most human of all the professions, and it is very hard to determine what success means when the challenge is to produce citizens with great character, a love of learning, and academic wherewithal.

Teaching is hard. Teachers already have so much on their to-do lists; seeking personal feedback to improve teaching in a systematic and explicit manner generally falls off their radar. A very real question teachers ask themselves is this: "Is doing one more thing—that does not directly involve my kids—worth the time?" Time is finite. Energy is finite. Is seeking feedback in a systematic way and analyzing the results really a good use of my time so I can better serve students? Although deciding to seek feedback may seem like an adult-centered decision at first glance, it is not—if the feedback is used to provide a better product for students. Therefore, the answer is yes. Seeking feedback and using it to improve practice is one of the most beneficial learner-centered strategies a teacher can use.

Example of Excellence

Mr. Mahoney is a second-grade teacher. His school has divided his schedule in a traditional way in which he is with the same students the vast majority of the day, every day. Mr. Mahoney has become known as the data expert among his team of teachers and is also known for his constant analysis of his performance and his student's performance. Interestingly, Mr. Mahoney never says the word "data." He simply talks about information and the gathering of information. He has found when he talks to kids or parents about collecting data, their eyes gloss over, but when he says he needs to get as much information as possible so he can do his job in the best possible way, they listen.

Mr. Mahoney gathers three types of information: the information that is naturally created through typical school activities, the information he can gather from those he is in contact with, and the information he can provide himself through reflection, documentation of actions, and self-evaluation.

It starts with his assessment of student progress, which happens daily. He always collects and breaks down the data in a manner to help guide his decisions in terms of how to continue to instruct the whole class as well as how to instruct individual students. He also keeps a running record of the instructional strategies he uses paired with the objectives students were to learn to see if certain strategies yield better results holistically for a class of kids. In past years, he has found different classes prefer to learn in different ways, so he made the necessary adjustments.

Next, he asks everyone he can think of for feedback in any way he can. He notes that if he were teaching AP, he would do the same thing, but the questions he would ask would notably look different. At the end of each week and chapter or unit, Mr. Mahoney now asks his students questions like, "When was learning the most fun?" and "When was the moment you knew you got it?" He asks their parents questions like "Were your children more or less excited about learning this week than usual?" and "What part of their learning were your children most excited to share with you?" Mr. Mahoney admits the sophistication of the questions is not otherworldly, but the data, excuse me—information—he can pull from the questions is invaluable. He notes that regardless of what questions he asks, people will also provide any information they feel pertinent. Mahoney actually said, "Asking the questions on a regular basis opens up the doors of communication and often times the most useful information is that which I did not even think to ask for."

Although the information he gathers from those methods has benefited him greatly in his journey to continually advance his professional practice, Mr. Mahoney notes that he learned more about his practice by watching a video of himself. He noted that this was a terribly uncomfortable process at first, but it has forced him into being comfortable evaluating himself. He also noted that this process makes evaluations by administrators and parents sitting in on his class not scary at all—"Because there is no way they can be harder on me than I am on me."

Why This Is a Learner-Centered Strategy

All teachers work hard. All teachers want to be great at their job and to serve their students. Few teachers take the time and take the risk to see if their hard work is having the impact they *hope* it is having. Taking the time to gather as much information (data) from as many different sources as possible to *confirm* whether or not what you are doing is successful is the epitome of taking the extra step to be truly student-centered.

Elements of Seeking Feedback to Remain Learner-Centered

Seeking feedback in any manner in the world of education is a great idea. In fact, it is difficult to think of a scenario in which an educator's attempt to receive feedback on his or her performance would be anything but positive and student-centered. In the following sections, we'll provide some relevant examples of how you can begin to employ this practice if this is something new to you. We'll look at three kinds of data:

- ◆ Naturally-created data
- ◆ Intentionally-created data
- ◆ Self-created data

Naturally-Created Data

The traditional act of "doing" school creates a lot of information. In fact, multiple times every day, in every classroom, information (data) is created that great teachers capture and then analyze to influence their upcoming actions. Throughout this book, there has been much discussion regarding how and when to collect and analyze data. There is nothing new or groundbreaking that this section should add, except for the fact that the data should be analyzed through multiple lenses. The first is to look at the material to assess the progress of the students in the class. The second is to take a deeper look at personal instructional success.

Assess Instructional Success

The collection of data and its use moving forward would always seem to be used to measure instructional success—and it typically does so in a manner designed to diagnose what kids did and did not learn and how to make subsequent instructional decisions. It is also important for teachers to measure the instructional success of their methodologies. This is an easier task for teachers who do not teach self-contained elementary classes, but is possible for all.

If a high school math teacher prefers to teach with graphics, direct instruction, and PowerPoint to support instruction and is trying to determine if this (her personal preferred means of instruction) is the most viable for students, she can simply teach one section of geometry in this manner and the next section using a different technique—perhaps a focus on manipulatives. The intent of this controlled experiment is to gather data to make better planning decisions in the future. The data created from this controlled experiment will influence how she remediates and intervenes with students, but also (after multiple repetitions and synthesis of data) allow her to better assess the true viability of both instructional methodologies.

The same can be done at the elementary level; it is just a more longitudinal process. A running record of student proficiency after initial instruction must be kept, and after a significant amount of data is collected, a finding can be made. According to the table in Figure 11.1 (page 96), it seems as though blogging has the best impact on Mr. Starkey's third-grade classroom, and lecture/discussion has the smallest benefit. Given this information, Mr. Starkey will adapt his go-to instructional style to focus on the method students are learning from best, not on the one he is most comfortable planning for and using to deliver instruction.

Intentionally-Created Data

There is much information within a school and school community that is not typically collected because it is not asked for that often. If a teacher truly has the mindset of "how can I work to make myself better?" then he or she has a myriad of options. Unfortunately, only great educators take advantage of these options. If you truly want to seek feedback in a learner-centered fashion, you should rely on three groups: colleagues, students, and parents. These groups have a vast knowledge of your strengths and areas for potential growth. Three simple ideas for procuring information from each of them are detailed on page 97.

Figure 11.1 Sample Running Record of Student Proficiency

Mr. Starkey's Third-Grade Language Arts Data Chart

Date	9/21	9/22	9/23	9/24	9/27	9/28	9/29	9/30
Strategy Used	Blogging	Lecture	Flipped Class Video	Blogging	Flipped Class Video	Lecture	Blogging	Lecture
% of students proficient on pre-assessment	21	27	30	33	19	35	17	25
% of students proficient on formative assessment after first instruction	77	59	62	81	74	58	89	64
Net Gain	56	32	32	48	55	23	72	39

Colleagues

◆ **Peer Observation and Evaluation**. This is the most intrusive way to gain information, but it is also generally the most effective. The vast majority of administrators love this concept, and if budgets allow, they will generally count this as PD time and provide a substitute.

◆ **Anonymous "What have you heard?" Surveys**. This is an idea that is generally administered throughout a team of teachers or even an entire school. Depending on the level of comfort and the dynamic between a faculty and staff, this does not need to be anonymous. However, also using an anonymous survey website can bring out information others may not normally feel comfortable sharing face-to-face.

◆ **Grade/Behavioral Comparison Charts or Conversations**. This activity mirrors the kind of activity normally associated with evaluating students to determine if they qualify for special education services. Through that process, colleagues get together and provide data to determine how to best serve a student. WHAT A GREAT IDEA! There is no need for a concern regarding student disability to exist before this can occur. One teacher can start this and gain data to see if in some cases he or she may be the issue with a certain child or if he or she has not employed a particular strategy that may be impactful. This activity calls for one teacher to ask a series of teachers to fill out a self-created worksheet to determine in what types of settings a student is either excelling or struggling.

Students

◆ **End of Unit Surveys**. Here are two tips for moving forward with this concept. 1) Before creating the survey, ask students what they hope that you ask them. This will help you create a survey to elicit better student responses. 2) If anonymity helps among professionals sharing information with professionals, then it will also help with students sharing information with their teacher

◆ **Suggestion Box**. This is a simple idea to employ, but it gives students a concrete mechanism for providing input on things they like and do not like. It is also very possible to create an electronic suggestion box that will allow for anonymous entries (without students being exposed through their handwriting).

◆ **Tap into Creative Thought**. Teachers can create systems of hearing feedback on their lessons. The question, "How could I have made this lesson/chapter/unit better for you?" calls upon students to tap into their creative thought and in most cases demonstrate understanding of the content in order to make a strong case for how to improve instruction.

Parents

- ◆ **E-mail Questions**. This is a great way to connect with parents before a student begins to struggle. For example, send a simple e-mail noting, "It seemed like Phil did not truly get the material today in class. I will try this strategy tomorrow to help him learn, but can you keep an eye on the situation and let me know if he shares anything with you?" This e-mail is short, shows that you care about students individually, empowers the parent, and asks for open-ended feedback. It's a win on multiple levels.

- ◆ **Parent-Friendly Surveys**. Educators often forget that parents are not educators. When seeking feedback, ask questions accordingly. Ask questions about their child and not the content.
  - • **Good Example**: Was there anything in particular in this unit that Mary seemed to like or discuss more than usual?
  - • **Bad Example**: The data indicated that the instructional strategy of questioning and discussion was used on 4/13 with limited success. Did your child also seem to struggle in mastering the word chunk "ink" that was taught that day?

- ◆ **Open-Ended Social Media Inquiries**. Hopefully all teachers attempt to engage their students' parents where they already are at—which in many cases is social media. A simple post or Tweet that reads, "Tried something new in class today. Did any of the kids mention if they liked it?" not only informs the parent, but also gives them something to directly ask their child to better involve them in their education. The response to the typical parent question, "How was your day?" is usually "Fine." The answer to the question, "Hey, I heard that Mr. Teipel did something new in class today—what was it?" will generally provoke a more than one-word answer.

Self-Created Data

Video, video, video. There is simply no better way to inform your instructional practice than to watch yourself on film. As humans, we are great at creating our own reality for ourselves that may not be true. This prevents that. For example, how many of you have been prompted to start a diet after looking at yourself in an unflattering picture? The image you saw looked right back at you in the mirror for weeks or months before that picture provided a moment of clarity. If it is possible to build up such a case of denial or altered reality that the image appearing in the mirror each morning can be denied, then what is possible with teaching? To truly demonstrate full commitment to improvement and seeking feedback in order to benefit students, there is one simple, two-part answer:

1. Video yourself.
2. Watch that video with a colleague and provide an evaluation.

If you consider all the other suggestions and tips provided in this book, but you do not feel a sense of urgency for change, then try one or two "film sessions," which will dramatically help guide your decision-making process as to in what ways you could best serve your students by becoming more learner-centered.

Moving Forward: For Kids

As we worked on this book, one thing burned in our core throughout: almost all teachers went into education because they truly wanted to benefit and serve children. As the world of education continues to evolve or devolve, it seems that sometimes the practices exhibited in many classrooms do not align with the core purpose and beliefs that teachers held when they first made the wonderful decision to work with and for kids. Merely "doing" school has led to decisions, some institutional and some made at the classroom level, that seem to exist for the benefit or convenience of adults as opposed to for the betterment of children. This practice may not be intentional or even realized by many who demonstrate it. However, it loses sight of the fact that all decisions in a classroom should be made in light of the best way to serve students.

This book is intended to support teachers in understanding what learner or student-centered instruction is and to provide a framework for moving forward in that vein. This is not intended to be a turn-key solution but instead a reminder of why we all want to become great educators. We also wanted to provide some support in making adjustments in practice if need be. Undoubtedly, some of the best thoughts and examples of how to make a classroom student-centered will come from the readers of this book and not have been provided by us—and that means that our mission was accomplished. It means that those teachers coming up with their own creative solutions have embodied a truly student-centered mindset that will help them adapt or transform their practice and hopefully that of the colleagues around them.

In the end, this book is about one thing: Every decision you make in terms of planning, instruction, analysis, classroom management, you name it—absolutely anything to do with the educational process—must be centered on the student. You can do this. You will be even more successful in the classroom. You will make an even larger difference in the lives of children.

Blackline Masters

First-Day Survey

1. What did your favorite teacher do differently to make him/her your favorite?

2. What did your least favorite teacher do differently to make him/her your least favorite?

3. When a teacher teaches something and you learn it very quickly, what is he/she doing that is different than the rest of the time?

4. When a teacher teaches something and it is hard for you to learn, what is he/she doing that is different from the rest of the time?

5. What is the best part about working in groups? What are the qualities of other students that you work best with?

6. What is the worst part about working in groups? What are the qualities of other students that you do not work well with?

7. Do you learn well on a computer? Tell me about something you learned and why it was easier on the computer.

8. Describe what you think of school in one word.

9. What is one thing I really need to know about you to be the best teacher to you that I can be?

10. When you get frustrated with learning a new concept, how would you like the teacher to interact with you—leave you alone for a minute, talk to you in the hallway, work with you individually inside the class, let your parents know so they can help you, etc.?

WWH Graphic Organizer

Outcome statement: As a result of this lesson, students will be able to . . .	
What does that really mean?	
Why is that important for us to know in this unit?	
How could we be asked to show that we understand that statement?	

Tic-Tac-Toe Lesson Board

Planning in Five-Minute Phases

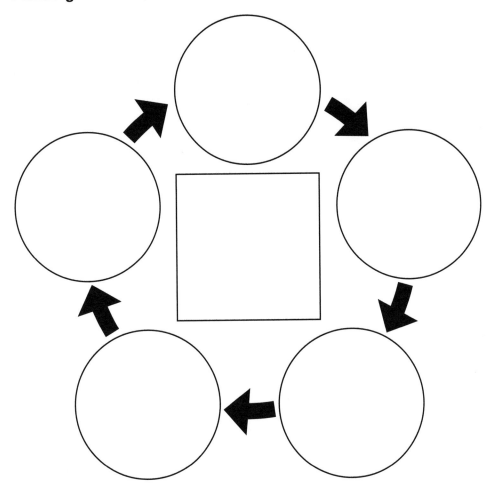

Classroom Rules vs. Guidelines

Write your rules in the left-hand column and rewrite them as guidelines in the right-hand column

Rules	Guidelines

Works Cited

Dufour, R. (2009, October 8). *4 critical questions of a PLC*. Bloomington, IN: Solution Tree.

Marzano, R., & Kendall, J. (1998). *Awash in a sea of standards*. Denver, CO: McRel.

Pink, D. (2009). *Drive: The surprising truth about what motivates us*. New York, NY: Riverhead Books.